Cover photograph by George Tomic Platform 7, Perth Central Station, *hand coloured fibre based silver print, 1998.*

54 149 775

Published by Arc Publications
Nanholme Mill, Shaw Wood Road
Todmorden, Lancs. UK OL14 6DA

First published in Australia in 1999 by
Fremantle Arts Centre Press
PO Box 158, North Fremantle
Western Australia 6159.
http://www.facp.iinet.net.au

ISBN 1 900072 40 8

Consultant Editor Wendy Jenkins
Production Manager Cate Sutherland

Typeset by Fremantle Arts Centre Press
and printed by PK Print, Hamilton Hill.

Yorkshire Arts

Arc Publications acknowledge financial assistance
from Yorkshire Arts.

Publication of this title was assisted by the
Commonwealth Government through the Australia
Council, its arts funding and advisory body.

Landbridge

CONTEMPORARY AUSTRALIAN POETRY

edited by John Kinsella

ARC
PUBLICATIONS

To the memory of John Forbes

CONTENTS

CONTENTS

CONTENTS

Contents

CONTENTS

INTRODUCTION

Australian poetry is rapidly finding a place in the context of an international poetics. It is considered by many Australians and non-Australians to be vital and unique, and one of the 'growth areas' of English-language poetry. This anthology has come together out of a desire to identify the diversity and energy of Australian poetry, and to show how the development of individual voices into the next century will contribute to a collective poetics.

I have no interest in restating the history of 'Australian poetry' as is done in many anthologies, nor in the process of appending Aboriginal oral traditions to just over two hundred years of post-settlement poetries to create some kind of nation-making canon. The risk of cultural insensitivity and of further colonisation renders this problematic. Australian poetry, from the point of view of this anthology, is a geographic and psychological entity rather than a purely historical one. If the poet is from Australia, lives in Australia, or perceives him or herself to be part of Australia, however they might envision it, then they should be considered for inclusion.

From this starting point I have looked to those poets who are likely to develop and expand their oeuvres into the next century, who are likely to contribute to the language in some energetic way, given favourable conditions. I have no specific inclination toward the experimental or the formal, and in fact am most interested where the two meet. I often find the experimental where it's not supposed to exist, and strong formalist tendencies in the reputedly avant-garde. So the binary is upset, even irrelevant from the outset.

The reader will find many of the established 'names' writing Australian poetry today — including Les Murray, Peter Porter, John Tranter, Dorothy Hewett, Fay Zwicky, Robert Gray, Gig Ryan, Kevin Hart, and Robert Adamson — in this anthology, as well as the names of those who've made relatively recent appearances but have already shown that they will contribute to the evolution of an Australian language and poetics

15

over the coming years — Alison Croggon, Peter Minter, MTC Cronin, Tracy Ryan, and many others. The anthologiser's guide to gender, ethnicity, and class, has been rejected for the linguist's guide to multiple and varied language usage — one usually finds that flexibility on this level allows for a less forced and more accurate reading of variety in these other 'categories'.

I have looked for language that is alive and vital, that adds something new to our reading experience, that escapes from the trap of telling the reader how a text should be read. This isn't a collection of identities, but of poems. The text wins hands down for me. Above and beyond everything else, each poet included has been given basically the same amount of space and been offered the opportunity to make a statement of intent and include a biographical note. This is intended to assist in moving with the poet's 'project' and to take the place of the canon-making pronouncements of the anthologist. I hope this volume, through the poets and their words, will dictate its own boundaries and determine its own fields of influence, or otherwise.

My intention has been to retain the integrity of regional identity and create lines of communication between regions, on a global scale — create an atmosphere of international regionalism. I want 'this' Australia to be read in an international context. I am interested in poets who represent aspects of the variable Australian voice. Whatever this might be, it's not fixed nor representative — diverse cultures merge to make it a growing and interactive language. As a consequence of the progressive nature of this anthology, it is with regret that some significant voices of recent years aren't included, such as those of Gwen Harwood and Philip Hodgins, whose deaths have meant a great loss for poetry in general. I have decided to include only those poets actively writing at the time of compilation. The late John Forbes, whose witty metaphysical poems (I note this term becoming increasingly associated with his work) have astounded more than one generation, and whose voice is undoubtedly unique in late twentieth-century English-language poetry, has been included as he was still alive while the volume was being compiled. We were able to discuss his selection personally, and this book is dedicated to his memory.

For me, the most significant voice to emerge in the latter years of this century is that of the Murri poet Lionel Fogarty. Fogarty has managed to use English as a weapon against its own colonising potential. He has created a positive hybrid that undoes the claim of linguistic centrality, and registers the primacy of the oral tradition. It is an integral part of the song cycle's development. In many ways his project of reclamation and autonomy, strongly political in nature, and dynamically active on the language level (if the two are even separable), has led me to see the necessity of an anthology that is active and operates outside the usual canonical guidelines.

As part of the regional integrity aspect of the selection I've looked across Australia rather than purely on the Eastern seaboard. In the end, however, I only included those poets I felt would also have appeal outside 'their' places. The book as a whole is interactive, something like a gallery space in which each work enhances our reading of another.

A few years ago I wrote an article for the *Australian Book Review* entitled 'Pulp Factions', in which I argued that the factionalism of Australian poetry was of little interest to the present generation of Australian writers. The divide between the so-called Generation of '68 and the 'Lehmann, Murray, Gray camp', the animosities between the poetry 'scenes' of Sydney and Melbourne, have been well documented elsewhere, and their signatures presented in a number of anthologies. Suffice it to say, that wonderful poets come from both sides of the 'divide/s', and that such animosities arose for concrete reasons, but they are of relatively little concern in the scheme of things. New rivalries and divides will appear and have appeared. Philosophical differences and questions of style and form abound, but these are endemic in any time. Difference is healthy as long as it generates debate. Many of the poets included in here were of those 'wars', but many aren't. I'd like to collect them under a new banner: Australian poets exploring Australian languages.

The internet has already become the most significant medium for the internationalisation of Australian poetry. In running the 'Poetry etc' international poetry email discussion list, I've noted the enthusiasm with which poets and critics from other cultures have responded to the geographic, demographic, and cultural particularities of Australian poetic voices. There is a fascination with the variety and breadth, the fact that it's not all 'wheat, sheep, and kangaroos' or 'Sydney'. Not that people don't look for those aspects too! But there's an admiration for Australian poetry's flexibility and fluidity. It is seen as a growth area.

The net has overcome such obvious problems as the difficulty of achieving overseas publication, and the expense of overseas communication. For all 'isolated' cultures it has been a boon. Obviously access isn't universal, but it is increasing. It's worth mentioning the excellent Australian literature site *OzLit* and that hypertextual growth area that does so much for creating an international space through which Australians might move with poets from elsewhere: John Tranter's web magazine, *Jacket*.

The culture of the literary journal is of particular interest to me, and quite a few of the poems selected in this anthology were first seen in literary journals, with a number coming from the journal I edit, *Salt*. Australia has had a fairly dynamic literary magazine culture, but one extremely vulnerable to the vagaries of federal and state government funding. The 'big' journals such as *Meanjin*, *Southerly*, *Westerly*, *Island*, and *Overland* have been solid and reliable despite their funding ups and downs, while newer journals such as *Siglo*, HEAT, and *Cordite* have maintained an atmosphere of cultural integrity and artistic potential. Above and beyond everything else, a literary journal culture is integral to the vitality of poetry and language itself. These are the testing grounds and places for juxtaposition and comparison. The crucibles of the word.

One of the most commonly imposed divisions, not only within Australian poetry but within Australian society in general, is that between the country and the city, the rural and the urban. The Boeotian–Athenian playoff that's been going on in Australian criticism, using the Murray–Porter model, since the '70s, has got a little long-in-the-tooth, and I'm sure both poets would be frustrated by the reductive nature of the model as it is haphazardly applied by critics in various circumstances. The idea that Murray represents one school of thought and Porter another has been a division of convenience. I have no interest in this. Murray is obviously a poet concerned with the rural, but he is also a linguist and is not averse to using the language of science and mechanics in his poetry. Porter, urbane sophisticate, is richly versed in the pastoral inheritance. Critics use polarities to divide and conquer. It's the poets' voices we are listening to here.

In many ways, it is possible to read Australian poetry through and against the landscape, rural and pastoral models. I'm using 'pastoral' here in the sense of the urban construct of the rural myth — as opposed to a specifically rural poetry. The Australian 'bush' identity is as much a construct of the city as it is of bush balladeers and singalongs around the campfire under the Southern Cross. It is at the core of our national identity, the propaganda that has so effectively excluded outside interaction and marginalised indigenous peoples. As 'British' and 'Irish'-ness become Australianness in the poetry of Harpur and Kendall — the Australian landscape comes into its own — we recognise the moves toward an eventual consolidation of national identity.

The work of the poet David Campbell has been used to emphasise this transition, and inheritance. But, as I've suggested, this is also a process of exclusion. Assimilating and absorbing landscape is the signifier for an Australian poetics, as it is for its art and culture generally. It's not surprising that the language of landscape should underlie much of our verse. And it is present in the work of many of the poets included here — Murray, McMaster, Hewett, Adamson, and so on. Even when not referring to it directly, the Australian poet is most often conscious of its overwhelming presence. John Forbes, however, argued that Australians, having a nostalgic vision of their independence and wealth coming from the wool on the sheep's back, forget the great contribution made by the 'city' to the Australian identity. But I'd argue that he and poets like Peter Porter and Gig Ryan are urban pastoralists whose poetry is deeply informed by this signature, even if they work against it. Once again, what specifically interests me is the crossover territory between different kinds of poetry. Between the rural and urban are the fringes, and the fringes produce the most interesting hybrid languages.

So, whereas anthologies tend to be retrospective or attempt to capture the identity of a particular theme or time, it is actually my aim in this volume to look to the future, to look towards these hybridising zones. There is a millennial fervour to capture the essence of modernity and to package it neatly — the *conceptual* rubicon formed by the year 2000 will prove to be exactly that. The effects of 2000 are, I'd guess, more to do with approaching it than passing it. This anthology is not so much prompted by a potential new poetics accompanying a new millennium as by the inherent movement in poetry regardless. And this movement need not be 'progressive', nor on a broad scale. It might be personal or cumulative, it might be a return to the traditional or an engagement with an avant-garde.

This is not to say that the demographics of poetries haven't changed with the times, because they have. The internet in particular has not only increased the potential of the 'amateur' poet to participate as poet in a 'public' space, but also the potential to collaborate and interact. The defusing of the 'lyrical I' throughout the '70s, '80s and '90s, particularly in American poetry, has reinforced a tendency to a polymorphous 'voice'. Poets have become conscious of how central they are, as individuals, to the pulse of the language they use. Some reject the need to move away from the 'I', and have dug in against linguistically innovative verse such as that of the American Language poets, asserting that the emotive authority of the self is at the core of what constitutes poetry, and that all attempts to move away from this are misguided.

On the other hand, the elevation of language to a thing-in-itself, providing its own terms of reference, being simultaneously the signifier and signified, has become a distinctly political process. And in the same way that the Language poets 'grew' out of a reaction to a society that engendered the Vietnam War and Watergate, linguistically innovative poetries in many languages and places have associated themselves with a movement away from the empowering, and consequently oppressive politics of self — the freedoms of the individual being best asserted, on this view, through an analysis of what constitutes the ego I.

Australian poetry in the late twentieth century — at least that available in the mainstream press and in literary journals — has tended to skirt these issues. Innovation has mainly come within the traditions of the 'lyrical I' poem — working within or against the lyrical and/or narrative structure. There's an important epistemological difference to be noted here. A poet like Robert Adamson with his radical poem of the early '70s, *The Rumour*, was working within the conventions of normal poetic expression. The concepts he examined may have been radical but the deployment of language wasn't. The words worked in a specific linear way. They didn't define themselves, or generate their own meanings — at least on a macro level. One could say the same of John Tranter's *Red Movie*, a revolutionary work in the Australian context in its systematic defamiliarisation of the object. Like much of Tranter's work it is concerned with the social politics of the material. It examines the processes of visual, verbal, and ultimately cultural fetishisation. Innovation has always been part of a developing poetics, but it hasn't been until more recent years that signs of what we might call the 'linguistically innovative' — a term I originally acquired from translation texts though claimed by a number of anthologists and critics — have become more common in both Adamson's and Tranter's work, and among Australian poets on a broad scale. An increasing number of poets have begun to focus on language itself, and its means of production — Wendy Jenkins and Peter Minter are strong representatives of this tendency. The historic links in an Australian context possibly include Anna Wickham, Christopher Brennan, Harry Hooton, and Francis Webb.

All in all, I've tried to make this the poets' anthology. It's not a definitive statement, and there are many other poets I'd like to have included. I haven't highlighted any individual poems, not because there aren't stunning pieces that leap off the pages in here, but since there are so many and each poem succeeds in its own technical terms — I feel these are all well-crafted pieces. Finally, what's made this a particularly exciting volume from my point of view is that many of the poets took up the offer to submit new, uncollected poetry for consideration. In many cases, poets are represented by one or more 'fresh' poems, in addition to the tried and tested pieces, stressing the forward-looking nature of the project as a whole.

John Kinsella, 1999.

ROBERT ADAMSON

There are two kinds of poetry in my first books, poems that were drawn from memory, basically descriptions of reality, and poems made up from art and the imagination. Since *Canticles On The Skin* (1970), I have been trying to work out what is real and what is imagined. Writing poems that escape intelligence 'almost successfully'. Of course you have to be Wallace Stevens or Michael Palmer to do that sort of thing but every poet who is aware of the limitations of language, of how impossible it is to describe reality, has the ability to transcend words and somehow build poetry from them.

I think from now on I will be writing love poems and elegies, trying to make sense of life by offering praise, looking for grace in the meaning of meaning, pushing my eyes into the light. 'The Night Heron' is a poem combining both a description of reality and elements drawn from art; it was inspired by Bob Dylan's *Time Out of Mind*. Crafting poetry from words seems to help deal with wonder and grief. Nothing is easy, there is no meaning except song, and song is not enough to bring the dead back without painful consequences.

ROBERT ADAMSON

The Night Heron

Midnight, my mind's full of ink tonight,
I'm drawing up some endings to make
a few last marks. Life's complete.
You're just a part of the mix,
a pain cocktail, dash of white spirit,
some pulvules of dextropropoxyphene
swallowed with black label
apple juice, as I cut and paste my past.

Life is sweet. Out there the night,
the stars in Technicolour, a half moon —
two half moons, the black branches
of a mangrove tree. Jasmine's
heavy in the hot air. I feel alright
even here suspended in a humid room
with another summer to get through.
I write down words, they all seem fake,

so I crack them open. A night
writing letters to the future and the past,
if you could look into the present
you might see this pudgy figure at the desk
throwing back double shots of gin,
fumbling for cigarettes and a light
writing the word 'political' in a black
thin calligraphy. Wearing a pair of digital

blinkers set on zero. Outside the night
heron swings in from the heavens,
and cuts through the aluminium light.
See its cream under wings, grey breast
the grey overcoat, watch it hit the pocket
of hot air, listen as it wheels on silence,
glides over the black calmness of swamp
and lands collecting with the creek.

The Drum of Fire

Out the back my father burning off,
drums of scrap, the lead casing
dripping from the copper wire —
toxic black smoke billowing into the air
each weekend, the lead trickling
down, molten rivulets spiting fire,
becoming deformed ingots.
His fuming shadow looming over
the neat rows of vegetables.
Weekdays I returned to school at night,
cutting through the alphabet,
torching examination papers, drunk
on fumes of kerosene, my fingers
lightening strokes. At morning
assembly we sang the national anthem
flat with deadpan faces — I blew
into a flute for a whole term and wept
each night poisoned by arithmetic
homework. Then down at the Police Boys
I boxed with bigger kids until
my head bled; in the park
I flew with the rainbow lorikeets
and hung upside down in the branches
of flowering coral trees. I sucked
nectar with them and stole their feathers;
I prowled back lanes with a pair
of claws that had dried into spiky stars
in my pocket. Back home I'd stare
into my father's drum of flames —
conjuring images of the new Ford Thunderbirds
that came purring through our suburbs,
and found no meaning in my father's fire
as he stashed another ton of copper wire.

Waving to Hart Crane

Farewell to the wire,
the voices on
the line. Goodbye
switchboard rider, my

American friend.
We enter the new
century through glass,
black oceans

and black winds,
thin fibre funnelling
poetry out
of existence.

No sonnet will survive
the fax on fire,
out-sound that hash
of voices slung up

from the cable.
Tip your hat
and flicker with
smoke from silent movies,

there are no more
clever gaps left
on the cutting room
floor by cunning editors.

Here they expunge
the message, nothing's
praise. If gestures
appear they fold in fade-out.

No River, No Death

1

Awake after years; sudden exploding mangroves,
alight as Mooney vanishes in mountain shade —

Late afternoon, confusion of words, language
alive with a life of its own, lashing

out and then licking its flesh wounds.
Words of the river, swarming here, in branches

of mangrove with prawn birds and fruit bats;

and mullet, butting upstream, schooling
leaping, and bull-nosed singing mullet songs —

Silver green needs spun till the spawn is done.

On the tide's line, a torn wing of sting-ray
waves in wash, prawns fester on the underside.

Now leave from a jetty, souls going where souls go;
the world's a mudbank in a dank westerly —

and there's nothing to hand, nothing to hold,
death's all around streaked in the afternoon air.

2

Here with the spirits of river gods, the lost,
lost in a holy place, its histories

entangled with sadness, deep sorrow in the rotting
wing and the remembering mangrove's core.

Over this planks, cut from swamp, return again,
hewn from trunks in their green years

now creaking complainers in the dull sun.
The wharf sags with tar-drenched oyster racks.

3

Nets circle the mullet school, the fishermen
shake their mesh and the old rope stings

the stumped fingers and crocked thumb,
then the fish buck under and die

in the net's wing lock; like a cloak cast
out from the fishers' minds the green tide's

gone black and the mullet are done,
hauled to their death from the spawning run.

4

Now here in a creek on Mooney Bay all river life
calms the head that's filled with news

of politicians oceans away, the death men:
whose voices rattle like loaded dice,

microwaved down to our side of the planet —
a sickness infecting the silt of this sacred tide.

War-headed malformation of the intellect:
an eyeless reaper, its cloak space-fabric

its titanium blade, its skull powdering radium,
the crippling power of crab-thought

turning its claws into its own back-flesh.

Though to feel it here, in the ancient river's
heart, with nature alive in a crawling

flying prehistoric line drawn on a rock.
Here in the belly of the serpent's beginnings —

is to know we may not go where all souls go,
hope's dead hearted in the name of science.

5

We will live with the threat of that white flash
until again like the hawks we gamble

with flesh, with oblivion — talons of the soul
along the heart in oblivion's blood,

and tear in the thin blue wind the black heart
out from the cave of our own sick heads.

6

The afternoon's last light has gone under now,
a flying fox swims in through a star

and the catfish are pecking the sting-ray's wing,
the larrikin prawn bird starts to sing.

ROBERT ADAMSON

Wild Colonial Boys

Musk ducks and the plump Wonga pigeon
were knocked from the sky
in blood sport, left to rot, then afterwards
in firelight were the games,
all various forms of gambling. In the mist
you'd hear knuckle-bones rattle
in their cotton pockets; or darned
in conversation, obscene words, slurred
by badly brewed alcohol; never song
but garbled recitations, coughed half-chants.
Whatever fed the imagination
was like a yellowness, it showed
in diverse activities: from plucking
ducks to the way they slept in postures
of loose decadence. The river
was a flood of their refuse, a smear of thick
waste through the countryside.
After storms and at low tide you'd see
the details of their hate; the score, a tally
and what they called their stake;
the sacred remnants of the ancient tribe's estate.

ADAM AITKEN

At the moment, my poems are increasingly influenced by where I live. With a feeling for 'negative capability', and an urge to include as much as possible about local history, and its Aboriginal heritage, I have been trying to build up a portrait gallery and land/seascape of characters who, I hope, can be recognised as local personalities. They may be metaphors for 'society', but also mirrors in which we can see the Self. My focus on the local may surprise readers: my best-known poems tend to describe what critics see as an Asian-influenced iconography. That is true to an extent — half my first book grew from an intensive period of time spent with my mother's family in Thailand. The other half were my 'Newtown' poems. Similarly, my second book has interested readers who were looking for whatever new geographical spaces I was exploring, and how the unity of the book brought these spaces together. So my present interest in the local may be because I have become sensitive to the charge that Australian poets travel too much, as if they could only find their subject within the novel culture of the Other. I am a product of my time — too old for Generation X, on the cusp with late baby-boomism (I remember watching TV reports on the end of the Vietnam War). Travel, backpacking, or tourism furnish a lot of the surface material for my newer poems, but the poems ought to reveal their own logic, and so I tend to see the irony in the whole process, being acutely aware that the traveller creates his or her own spectacle and creates a provisional notion of the authentic. My work challenges the notion of 'national' literature, since my subjects could exist in one of many metropolitan centres; television, advertising, thirty-second sound bites, jump cut music videos, globalised culture are all grist for my own particular mill. Still, I believe that under all the plastic, the post-modern pastiche, that pretense of consumer liberation that wipes out the corner shops of the local, a spirit of resistance waits to come up to take a long, deep, and lyrical, breath of air.

ADAM AITKEN

Easy riders

Sunday hymnals
welcome us
but we ignore them
trailbiking with ever greater
recklessness
further into the breeze.
Belief hits top gear
just past the weatherboard
chapel, miniature ports
and hand pumped petrol
and trails that end
in limeburnt
gullies of karst.
Hawaiian shirted foreign animists
swerve through an ancient bridge collapse
and revive the art
of motorcycle maintenance —
instant first aid
in the shadow of a Banyan tree.

Symbiosis

We sit in conference
holy ghosts chaired in stone.

We consider whether
human flesh really
tastes very nice

and if so
which parts
are the tenderest.

We thought it rude
to ask, and paid for what
we got:

a man with a hat
and brilliant embroidery
dyed in human blood
collecting money
for the dance:

his Marlboro-smoking
Sigale-gale puppet
and an art hungry audience
of Swedes, freshly tattooed
joining in the fun.

Marxist Theme Park Budapest

for Chris Kelen

1

Monoliths welcome the overcast day
on scrubby fowl yards east of Pest.
No dawn, no dusk.
'Look forward to a walk in the graveyard of capitalism'
my English host writes in the visitors' book.
We goosestep through the entrance gate, in time
to a thirties workers' hymn on an old valve wireless.
At the ticket box I find the retro-chic you like:
East German design classics
and check my wad of florints, khaki cash of dreams.

We promised to buy, but for years they wouldn't sell.
Now they sell, Lenin's side show T-shirt,
the canned Last Breath of Marx
giftwrapped for a friend.

Your name a suburb here: Kelenfold.
Boring, I thought, my feeling for it all it's worth,
but think how language
(your father's first and now his second)
makes a difference! Kelen Senior
who's learning IBM function keys
dreaming in Hungarian perhaps.

2

But from this distance I hear
the Kelen version of Kokoda, as you tell it,
a larrikin's lark. (Sent to guard a jungle track,
he looked bad hiding up a tree, tripping on datura,
watching his counterpart, the corpse of a Jap sniper,
dead three days.)
Let's not fear the dead, but go
and love them. So Creon said.
My favourite statues? Macquaries and explorer thieves,
sentinels at libraries or a court of law,
and school children recite their achievements,
unknown soldier at a bus depot, or the Winfield Cup,
rugby stars with a gold plated footy,
or the bronze boar at Sydney Hospital.

3

In a fallow paddock ten k's out of town
you won't need to shoot, your favorite saints
are concrete. Save your crowbars, hammers and chisels.
Poetry on a Cyrillic plaque.
Cliché corrodes
like acid rain on marble.

Soviet-Hungarian Friendship, an awkward phrase;
no poet could ever make that scan, whatever translation.
A problem fitting words to a dead occasion.
The Workers' Party Widows come,
grey hump backed Russian tanks, old tractors run on tears
whose advances end in friendly fire.
Terror inflected with a sigh, written on a moist cheek,
handfuls of wild daisies on a scaffold

of hearsay: who knew whom, who shot whom.
They lecture with a waving finger,
for the tour leader's video, a Sony's aimless panning.
Give them light, I thought
give them light and 4 track VCRs.
TV's final revenge. They remind you.

4

A little boy poses under a Cyclops
combing his hair under a giant thigh.
Nikon propped on biceps, someone locates
the infra red self-timer, and I say smile!
Nineteen seventeen, the workers lean into their work
with futurist umbrellas, acid-eaten flags
the size of aircraft ailerons, taking off
from a plinth tracered with trompe l'oeil bullet holes.

No head droops, no sadness here.
A face chiselled with grim belief.
The way they wear their art, these ferrous lies:
giants miming flight with spring at their feet
in a field of rusty stubble, clover and dandelion.

5

Two lovers hold hands, shivering and free.
March out of this grey weather, the cutting wind
toward sunshine.
Soft and emotional, we discover
concrete is portable as an Eastern breeze
placed with all due ceremony,
music and special stamps,
into a can.

ADAM AITKEN

Saigon The Movie

James Bond flies into Phuket, which he pronounces
Fukit and this announces the demise
of the colonial era.
My mother sits on the Left Bank, harvesting rice.
The Baron announces his arrival
with a slice of lemon between his teeth and
Panama with razors embedded in its rim, to wear
to restaurants with a view of crossfire.

The iron butterfly folds back her wings, and rests awhile
on the pillows of this city.
But they are soaked
with the formalin of diplomacy
and the perfumes of an irresistible corruption.

Finally the old merchants
dig up their gold and re-invest in a
coat of arms they wire to a security gate.
Guard dogs with degrees, and lap-dog breeds
that do not bark.
Here a childhood made sensitive to bombs,
a kindergarten closed down with prayer,
American linguists in a helicopter, dropping
ration packs of Chicklets and brand new grammar.

In One House

for Rick and Hugh de Ferranti

Back in a year you almost forgot
we lived in Surry Hills.
We also lived in Strawberry Hill, the pub
famous for a band competition you nearly won
with a song you called White Food.

36

Our terrace for dolls, with a stable for cows
and servants for the Lord and Lady Buckingham
up the road. Heaven and Hell packed out
the Trade Union Club. A piano packed with dust
yielded harmonies for those with ears
for a telephone's incessant ringing.
We'd rub, beat and bleach the laundry
until it shrunk to puppet size
to fit line of leg and arm, breast, hip and ankle.
We looked and felt ultra tight
marched two doors down to the brothel
(Visual Merchants Dream Society) and thought of signing up
then let down the tires of a Rolls Royce
belonging to the Spank Sportswear executive.
The fleas found us intolerant.
Three varieties of toast were memorised — brown,
burnt, incinerated.
The sun hurt so we stayed inside.
Some of us are still inside, feeding six kids
or labouring on some endless Ph.D
on an island of troubadours, all blind.
Some of us posted to a country needing diplomatic skills
we had mastered — the subtle
look that said we disapproved, the ease
we turned quite blind to strangers in our beds,
the double entendre at dinner
the crisis surrounding a shared bilingual lover.
But who then ever were — strangers I mean —
in a house of friends? We all knew then
who would make a fortune
advising governments what to do
always good at kitty, collecting
for the bills. Their equations just got longer
scored into the old pine table.
Some less lonely now, less curable,
refusing the rescue flares of darkness and the gloss
of victimhood
but here to stay like a generation
tagged on to the last, bemused by the next,
some still writing
poems to their friends.
Clean living under difficult circumstances
as the Mods used to say.

LISA BELLEAR

I won't compromise and why should I?

This is Aboriginal land. Our country was invaded some two hundred and ten years ago. As a writer, artist, activist, my work will always address these issues.

You can allow your eyes and heart to see. See the injustice, cruelty, and you can also hear the laughter and feel love.

I love this country, my home, although sometimes what I see, hear and feel, makes me cry.

I hope through my words any person can connect with many serious societal issues which must be addressed (if healing is to begin).

Women's Liberation

Talk to me about the feminist movement,
the gubba middle class
hetero sexual revolution
way back in the seventies
when men wore tweed jackets with
leather elbows, and the women, well
I don't remember or maybe I just don't care
or can't relate.
Now what were those white women on about?
What type of neurosis was fashionable back then?
So maybe I was only a school kid; and kids, like women,
have got one thing that joins their schemata,
like we're not worth listening to,
and who wants to liberate women and children
what will happen in an egalitarian society
if the women and the kids start becoming complacent
in that they believe they should have rights
and economic independence,
and what would these middle class kids and white women do
with liberation, with freedom, with choices of
do I stay with my man, do I fall in love with other
white middle class women, and it wouldn't matter if
my new woman had kids or maybe even kids and dogs
Yes I'm for the women's movement
I want to be free and wear dunlop tennis shoes.
And indigenous women, well surely, the liberation
of white women includes all women regardless …
It doesn't, well that's not for me to deal with
I mean how could I, a white middle class woman,
who is deciding how can I budget when my man won't
pay the school fees and the diner's card club simply
won't extend credit.
I don't even know if I'm capable
of understanding
Aborigines, in Victoria?
Aboriginal women, here, I've never seen one,
and if I did, what would I say,
damned if I'm going to feel guilty, for wanting something
better for me, for women in general, not just white

middle class volvo driving, part time women's studies
students
Maybe I didn't think, maybe I thought women in general
meant, Aboriginal women, the Koori women in Victoria
Should I apologise
should I feel guilty
Maybe the solution is to sponsor
a child through world vision.
Yes that's probably best,
I feel like I could cope with that,
Look, I'd like to do something for our Aborigines
but I haven't even met one,
and if I did I would say
all this business about land rights, maybe I'm a bit
scared, what's it mean, that some day I'll wake up
and there will be this flag, what is it, you know
red, black and that yellow circle, staked out front
and then what, Okay I'm sorry, I feel guilt
is that what I should be shouting
from the top of the rialto building
The women's movement saved me
maybe the 90s will be different.
I'm not sure what I mean, but I know that although
it's not just a women's liberation that will free us
it's a beginning

Beautiful Yuroke Red River Gum

for Northlands Secondary College Mobile Rebel School

Sometimes the red river gums rustled
in the beginning of colonisation when
Wurundjeri,
Bunnerong,
Wathauring
and other Kulin nations
sang and danced
        and
            laughed
                aloud

Not too long and there are
fewer red river gums, the
Yarra Yarra tribe's blood becomes
the river's rich red clay

There are maybe two red river gums
a scarred tree which overlooks the
Melbourne Cricket Ground the
survivors of genocide watch
and camp out, live, breathe in various
parks 'round Fitzroy and down
town
        cosmopolitan
        St Kilda

And some of us mob have graduated
from Koori Kollij, Preston TAFE,
the Melbin Yewni

Red river gums are replaced
by plane trees from England
and still
        the survivors
           watch.

Mother-in-Law

Took me thirty years before I left your father
Battered wife syndrome, well that's the term the
Social worker used at the neighbourhood centre
Oh I didn't realise I was being abused. On the bad days
I never left the house, told friends, not that I had many
I was visiting a relative who had taken poorly
Look at me sweetheart, you've made the right decision
Believe me, you have to think of Stacy, and don't forget
You have to take care of yourself. Mothers have rights
Mothers have needs too. I'll not make excuses for
Your behaviour, you have to work through that, nor
Can you say it was all Larry's fault. Honey don't cry
Together we'll be okay, you've got to stop hating yourself
Alright, the court order allows fortnightly access visits
On the proviso he's not been drinking — listen he's not
Doing right by you or Stacy, coming here drunk. He
Hasn't even bothered to shave. Darling, he may still care
He may even still love, but rules are there for the protection
Of the child, and for the sanity of the mother. Maybe the
Next time you will be able to welcome Larry inside but
For now, tonight, the situation, the reality is no, and if
He's still there in five minutes, Larry knows the score
There's a train, or there's a police van
It's up to him

Souled Out

Only $200 — Ladies/
Gents and you could
Become an Aborigine
For two whole days!
Hey lady, what's sar matter
Haven't you seen
One before?
Come and experience
The lifestyles and
Mystical spirituality
That is quintessential
To the life and existence
Of a Traditional Aborigine
We'll also have a real
Properly initiated Elder
Who will empower you
With Dreamtime secrets
From an ancient culture
And for an extra fifty bucks
We'll throw in some
Real live witchetty grubs
And eat them, just like
The Natives did all those
Dreamtimes ago.

Ode to Nelson Mandela

Why Mr President does your
ANC dominated government
which is conveniently based
on a patriarchal model
why Mr President do you
allow-sanction-not
question the continual
sale of arms to
the former Rwanda government
Why Mr President Why

Can you share with
me/us all colonised
peoples, all colonised
nations and 'oppressive'
'brutal' 'alien' 'coloniser
countries' just one
justification for your
government's sale of arms
to the Former members of
Rwandan government who
are now currently in Zaire
regrouping, reassessing the
Stage II plan

G for Genocide

… Mr President?

JUDITH BEVERIDGE

While I'm writing, I try as much as possible to forget about intentions, directions, aims and outcomes. I'm very grateful if by the end of a session of writing a poem, or even a few lines that strike me as pleasing begin to emerge. What I've learned over the years is to value patience and receptivity. For me, these states help prepare the ground for creative activity. Now, more than anything, it gives me great pleasure to try and engage with the subtle, musical components of language. I love texture and richness, yet I also love simplicity and directness. To have strong imagistic content combined with an exquisitely arranged music is what I'd like to achieve. Not so much what is written, but rather how something is written is what interests me most. My guides have been many along the way and here I will only acknowledge a few: Wallace Stevens, Amy Clampitt, Charles Wright, Galway Kinnell, Rilke, Elizabeth Bishop. I try to keep in mind that my activity as a poet is very privileged, very sophisticated. It is predicated upon great good fortune. So many people do not have access to literacy, or to the socio-economic conditions that could make writing a choice for their lives. It is important then, to recognise how sacred poetry is, how important, how rare. I have a responsibility, then, to bring to it the best I possibly can.

Making Perfume

So, that summer I picked everything:
the hibiscus that shut at six o'clock,
the white pollened flower
I called The Baker's Daughter,
the yellow rose that lasted weeks beyond its season
and the great pale flower with a cold look —
Queen in the Tower.

Then I took some bottles from their cupboards
and their lids twirled off and their perfume
came three voices high in my head.
I lined them like wineglasses on the sill
and filled each with petals and water
and gave them keyboard names like
Chandelier and Tier on Golden Tier.

I remember how I lived that summer
in a room with a thousand windows in blue and green.
I'd stay out late to pick and soak the petals
and pour them into bottles and bury them in the earth
with a made-up name for a simple flower plus water.
Later, I'd wash and line the bottles on the sill
and read their labels until each one rang

a terrace of bells in my head.
I mourned the bottles I named for my heroines of hopeless love
and stood them in kitchentapwater
and stored them out of the light.
I dreamt of balls, dinner roses,
a woman gently naming herself to herself.

Now, I wonder whatever happened to Lavinia,
the Fourteen Nights, Ballet Blanc,
the fragrance in the blue twirled bottle
I named Pirouette.
Months later I probably poured them down the sink.

But no-one suspected that summer
why my eyes were suddenly circled with a dark pencil,

why my cheeks had the faint flow of day,
why I swished my skirts as I moved.

I kept the bottles with me, moved them about the room
vowed not to open them for seven years,
and named them after the girl kept at home
who never stopped saying as she stirred her pots:
O, I wish, I wish, I wish …

The Domesticity Of Giraffes

She languorously swings her tongue
like a black leather strap as she chews
and endlessly licks the wire for salt
blown in from the harbour.
Bruised-apple eyed she ruminates
towards the tall buildings
she mistakes for a herd:
her gaze has the loneliness of smoke.

I think of her graceful on her plain —
one long-legged mile after another.
I see her head framed in a leafy bonnet
or balloon-bobbing in trees.
Her hide's a paved garden of orange
against wild bush. In the distance, running
she could be a big slim bird just before flight.

Here, a wire-cripple,
legs stark as telegraph poles
miles from anywhere.
She circles the pen, licks the wire,
mimics a gum-chewing audience
in the stained underwear of her hide.
This shy Miss Marigold rolls out her tongue

like the neck of a dying bird.
I offer her the fresh salt of my hand
and her tongue rolls over it
in sensual agony, as it must
over the wire, hour after bitter hour.
Now, the bull indolently
lets down his penis like a pink gladiolus
drenching the concrete.

She thrusts her tongue under his rich stream
to get moisture for her thousandth chew.

Incense

for my father

All day a fragrance —
as if the sun has lingered too long
over the bowl of old green apples.
Outside the sun has turned the leaves
more apricot, more amber.
The sparrows are robbing the sunflowers,
the spider tools a web white as signaler's smoke,
and at the day's soft centre
the bees find the smell of burning leaves
to turn their honey cinnamon.

And there, clutched at by the vines
the weeping rose leans
its thin frame into the wind
like a bare scarecrow, a dying saviour.
The leaves turn
their loose litter to the flames
to the ash
at the end of the summer's reign.

I remember the leaves tossing
those flames outwards like garlands
and the ash that fell like backyard stars
along the tops of roses.
And that fragrance takes me back
to some sour nostalgia out of childhood
where urine and turps made violets.

The day we stood burning the leaves.
They shed such grey exotic wastes.
We watched those little suns extract fragrance
out of hard dead splinters.

*

Now all I have are these sticks,
pickets that stake out your memory,
wands conjuring old stars
and the air filling with the smell of wood,
of laurel split for fuel.

With these dipsticks I test the dark
measure the oil left in the lamp
of affordable ruby — those roses
we watched the daylight dim by
as we fed their jossed blossoms to the fire.

*

You are gone, your ash is scattered
and these sticks just ghost your bloom.

But I remember the starlight,
the scent that trespassed,
the petal that opened, the red tip
that raised it all sweeter than it was.

The flames bloomed gold against the summer
and the weeping rose
we bundled into the fire
and all its windfallen blossoms.

*

In a confetti of ash and petals
I hunt out your memory.
In each decimal spark
in the moods beyond surveillance
I close my eyes to the tips
of infant roses,
to the smoke of burning leaves
uncurling like vines in an orchard
where light is the light of hillsides
in yellow May.

But in the betrayal of falling suns,
the thin stems eaten by red tips
on an insect time-scale,
stars drop and burn
tips grow amber with decay.
In a long red chamber
you are inner oils already burnt.

*

I watch the smoke move off
it lifts like light
it trickles like a hose
placed over a garden, over low flowers
that make perfect borders. I sit by
these stilts to stilt-walk in aerial wonder
at the earth, the water clutched at
by the vines, the rose weeping into the wind,
and the fruit-fly circling
each windfallen length.

To the Islands

I will use the sound of wind and the splash
    of the cormorant diving and the music
any boatman will hear in the running threads
    as they sing about leaving for the Islands.

I will use a sinker's zinc arpeggio as it
    rolls across a wooden jetty and the sound
of crabs in the shifting gravel and the scrape
    of awls across the hulls of yachts.

I will use the wash-board chorus of the sea
    and the boats and the skiffler's skirl
of tide-steered surf taken out by the wind
    through the cliffs. Look — I don't know

much about how to reach the Islands, only
    what I've heard from the boatman's song
and from a man who walked the headland
    to find a place in the rocks free of salt

and osprey. But perhaps I can use
    the bladder-wrack and barnacle, the gull
wafting above the mussels and the bird
    diving back to the sea. Perhaps I can use

the song sponge divers sing to time each dive
    and then use their gasps as they lift
their bags onto the skiffs. Perhaps
    the seapool whispers of the sun-downers

or the terns above the harbour are what
    the divers sing to as they hold their
breath and swim the silent minutes through
    with prayer. I will use the gull's height

and the limpet's splash and the wasps' nest
    hanging like a paper lamp under the pier
and the little boat sailing out. Even the
    fishermen lugging shoals over the stones,

even the sailors shift-walking the decks,
    even the end-blown note of a shell levelled
towards the horizon. I will use the eagle's
    flight moored in the eyes of children

and the voices of men, the ones, they say,
    who've made it, though perhaps the purlin
creaking on its rafter, the gull squawking
    from the jetty, the wind calling

along the moorings and the notes the divers
    hear in the quiet waters of their breathing
as they seek release through the depths
    are all *I'll* know about finding the Islands.

Meanwhile, I'll use the sound of sunlight
    filling the sponges and a diver's saturated
breathing in the lungs of an oarsman
    rowing weightless cargo over the reefs.

KEN BOLTON

I don't think I have a project, beyond attempting to be interesting. My poetics, negatively defined, would seek to avoid an image-laden, metaphor-driven writing as conventionally 'poetic' — i.e. dilly. The conventionally poetic, too, I think, precludes many subjects and kinds of discursive tone and I like mobility and number in these things — both as indices of, and means toward, a kind of immediacy of response and experience. I like poetry that seems selfconscious, epistemologically nervous.

I am also attracted to an aesthetics of the arbitrary and surprise — through the determinations of a restricting form or via collage — though these are not exampled in the present selection.

Mix and heterogeneity are what I like. I think the world is at least that complicated and that our responses to it are, too.

The things I do don't add up to a 'project', in my mind, though they are an attempt to reclaim intelligence and relevance for poetry, to operate outside the circumscribed space much of it normally and voluntarily inhabits, muted, sidelined, corny, an anachronism murmuring ruefully about its (non) status, a poetry of 'poetic' images, well rounded metaphor and the rest, 'experiences' turned effortlessly into epiphanic, realised lessons. Sufferin' succotash! 'I mean, am I being too harsh, Roy?'

Florence to Lorraine Lee

Dear Lorraine,
                    Cath & I have made it
to Florence
                    where, in part of it, I sit in
my undies
          (red)
                              at the 'bureau' (blond)
& write to you.
                    Cath sleeps
                                   just
behind me
                    looking comically
                                   like that
painting
          by Vuillard
                              that is chiefly grey
I think
          in which a few dark lines
                                   (black)
indicate a bed, in profile, small head at
one end
               & a peak rising at the other
where the feet might go
                         only this is
in brilliant white
               & looks like this

you will see
from this   her head
(beautiful, rested, a warm
colour)

is at the opposite end
from the Vuillard
picture
My life is different to his.

Pisa
was beautiful.
If I could be a painter

& there was any point in repeating, totally,
the
emotions of the past, I would paint that sweep
of buildings facing onto the river — from a spot
on the bridge over it
looking right.
(This
places the railway station somewhere at my back
a few blocks away
on the same side of the river
as I stand
— for your reference.
And it is
late afternoon.)
The water is a deep
spinach colour   that somehow has in it
much else
& the grand placid sweep of the buildings
is the Italian confidence
that they do it right

— what? —
build things, design, live.
They too,
the buildings,
are almost indistinguishable
from each other —
flat facades, the same

KEN BOLTON

                                                              three
windows at each height

                                        the buildings all as tall
as each other
                        & abutted, exactly. And their
colours
                are lovely   —
                                        chiefly, a range of mustard
yellows,
                        some ochres, some greys, a blue-grey, a
rose, a pallid, almost-white or two,
                                                some mauves,
but chiefly those ochreous yellows
                                        ranging from
jaundiced
                to a rich pumpkin orange confidence,

the pillars or pilasters around the windows
                                                in
dulled white & greys & bone
                                & in the windows: shadow —
melancholy, sad, or private …
                                        merely sleepy, or
inexpressive
                except to say, This is how it goes.

And overall the picture would say
                                Calm,
                                                        an
emphatic
                but understated
                                feast
                                        of — I don't know —
'disclosure', 'beauty', 'just proportion'

                                        Paris beauty
is so much
                more nervous, & fine-lined —
                                                        the
surface of French buildings
                                more articulated, the

56

beauty more lightly & shiftingly present

                       the

difference between

             Bonnard & Boldini

(If I have got the name right

                  — is he the Italian

who did society portraits

                  — family groups etcetera —

in London

        18th century?

                      a kind of bland-

ness

      that is direct —

             conservative — understatedly

forthright.

        I am pushing it here — all these

art references —

        who will get them?   Will you?

'Sweetie Pie?'

        Cath says. 'Would you

open the window?'

           & I do. A lovely park

is just outside

       & fills the window with

green green leaves

          the trees of the square below.

We are 3 stories up

       & look down on a square

— the noise of birds, wind

            in the leaves, motor scooters

& distant cries

      & now a bell. It rings for me

& rings for you, here.

                *

Well the poem ends there. I think I meant Batoni for the
painter (Goldoni & whoever are probably musicians). I meant
to write you a letter — but I had nothing to say so I thought
I'd write a poem & 'see what was in there'. Mostly clichés.

Some guy should send photos of Cath & others from her conference. Could you send them on?

I'll write properly from Australia. Meanwhile, thank you for
the stay in Paris.

Here we're in the *Andrea* hotel, whose owner we met at the
railway station — cheap, very nice, & on a square — across
which we look to the Duomo, which is just 2 blocks away.
We've drunk already at both *Il Patriarcho* (The Patriarch) & the
Genius Bar. Both okay.

An Empty Space

for Becky Davis leaving 'her place of employ'

'Glad To Be Unhappy' is the name
Of a jazz tune I like, but not as much as I
Like the title itself. It describes, for me, a state
          of luscious
Despond. I am not sure I ever experienced it — though
          I feel I have — 'phantom-limb' style.

When I think of it I think I think of the music on a particular
          Eric Dolphy
Album. With that track on it. — How circular.
That is not how I felt when I heard you were leaving: you told
          me, standing
Close by, at the traffic lights on Morphett Street — I
Had to stand apart. Must I continue to grow up, cast
          securities aside, be tough? Why, why must you go?

For a while I could not look at you
Or speak. 'What will happen to me?' is how I felt.
          I might even have said it —
Really, as a joke to you — but to tell you how I felt:

sad, I tell you. The tune is '2 4 5' I think:
'Glad To Be Unhappy' — I don't know how it sounds.

You should play it one day. I should tape it for you.
Oh god. Well, I admire you & think you're terrific
          — & like you immensely. You're off to the
Unknown. Where I could never tread. But I salute you
          — a corny attitude my heart strikes — like the earth-
          lings, looking into the sky, when the superior beings
          return to their galaxy, of whom they say, wonderingly,
          'Will they ever come back?' Would that you would —
          'there is room in the room I room in'   (joke). Room
          everywhere.

PETER BOYLE

Chiefly I would like my poems to satisfy my own taste for what seems a good poem, to give me the kind of pleasure in writing them that acts as both stimulus and highly fallible indicator that what I'm writing might work as a poem. Beyond that I would like my poems to say something, to make feelings come alive, to convey genuine emotions. I don't see my poems as experiments in pure aesthetics — but equally I don't want to produce propaganda or some kind of on-going autobiography. Within those very vague parameters I try to experiment with a range of forms and content. My own tastes largely come from what I've read and valued: European poets like Rilke, Supervielle, Mandelshtam, Akhmatova, Seferis, Ungaretti, Americans like James Wright, Levine, Kinnell, Elizabeth Bishop, Charles Wright, Wallace Stevens, Pound, Eliot, Hispanic poets like Lorca, Alberti, Vallejo, Neruda, Borges, Montejo, French Poets like Reverdy, Char and Bonnefoy — but that list is always open to addition and revision. Between reading, my own life and what happens out there in the world I'm hoping poems will continue to emerge that are both personally satisfying and different from what I've done before.

The Colours of Ageing

(Anacita's poem)

The avocados in autumn age under black skins,
their green smell like mossy stones under a waterfall.
In the kitchen reach out and touch
the smooth slime.
In my country we eat them with icecream
or tinned sweetened milk.
My father in his workday singlet
would leave his portion for me
and go out
to be alone with the chooks.
In the floral nightdress she wore all day
till the sun bleached the red from the roses
my mother is fussing and flailing.
Afraid of her hard hand
we rush out, my brothers and me,
to hide under the palm trees as the first rains come down.

All that was long ago.
The trees grow now in a different autumn.
Seen through winter frost a lone palm
rises out of excavated earth.
Derelict walls turn their backs on the sun
and I age under this skin of woven cloth.
The cicadas along the riverbank find nothing
except the black sleeves of their discarded livery.
Their shrill moan
traces in evening air
all that was green.

Cesar Vallejo

Dead these sixty years in Paris
where rain and snow once more
bury the hungry boulevards,
you stand head bowed
above what seems to be a gravestone,
the wide hat of a ranchero in your hand
and with the grimace of a man who loses all in a cockfight.
Amigo,
I hear the shrill song that flows under your breath.
In darkest nightmare summoning the names of all colours
you mutter so quietly
the savage diction of a cerebral chemist.

Or I meet you in the hospital
where polishers whirr
enormous circles on the moonlit floor.
The X-rays tacked up on the wall,
their dark scrawl
threading the pain of the earth to the pain of the stars.
A white bird drops by saying 'Open this door.'
The curtain of your sickbed waits to move
like the sail of a ship.
In Peru the horse of your childhood
still chews its grass, tosses its mane
in the last dryness of summer.
A poem or a life
ripples between such trivial and such portentous matter,
incorporates derision,
dispenses its own handshakes.

And if after so many words
not one word
And if among so many breaths
not one sigh
crosses the vacuum.

In a dream you woke to find the windowsill opposite your bed
lined with money,
little gold and silver coins that shone at you.

In the next room the same
and at the front door
a row of coins the same.

Such embarrassing gifts among bandaged heads.
Bloom of putrefaction on the skin
of the one who guards twilight.
Graced always with the wealth of the air,
Cesar Vallejo,
under Paris rain
seeking the correct and final gesture,
giving these aesthetic otherworldly objects
their human name.

A Winter Symphony

1

The river which flows to the edge of the sky —
you can see a shining in its depths
as if its light would enter your hands.

All along the bank the dead are burning.
A small girl is poking in more twigs
and a cat, smashed and gutted,
floats by in the icy flood
rolling steadily out of the mist.
Hung from wintry trees
mirrors rattle thinly.
How long ago did they make this place of burning,
these worn stones that take on
the shape of grief?
The river opens around you,
its brown lips against your chest,
its dark undercurrent caressing your thighs.
Here where fallen branches glide
deep waters move

and the smooth snow streaks with white
the tiny grey eyes of fish.

The long river tumbling over and over
roars beyond vision.
All that remains, the scattered ashes,
for how long do they drift,
a trail of grey dust on this river
that rushes on towards the sky?

2

My backyard where the rain
lances brief explosions of brightness in puddles
is a night sky where stars
are born and go out
at miraculous speed.
A rusted tricycle
performs the role of solar system,
the white curve of its wheels suggesting infinity.
Limp shirts on the line crowd the background,
waiting in evening drizzle
like the outer circles of paradise.

On such a night I imagine a man walking alone across Paris.
I see the clear cold of the lights in small bars,
the Arabic lettering growing faint
in a small alley —
this man so often transfigured
by the joy of sky and lights,
the crowds going in, the girls coming out,
the sense of life beginning
in chance encounters, rapid glances,
but this night all he sees
is the concrete shell of a room where the door is open
and no one enters.
The man — his name is Maurice Ravel —
has just started to notice
how the music his fingers place on the page
is not the music he hears —
some kind of wild shuffle

transposes his intentions.
He recalls three nights in a row
waking to the same dream —
it is summer
in the garden blossoming at his window
and the horn of a liner wakes him out of sleep on the ocean's floor,
his body alert but without movement,
paralysed by the beautiful play of the stars
refracted through so much water.

3

Saturday morning in the park.
He holds the ring of soapy water
up to the chill wind —
it lifts and breaks the bubbles.
A girl dances in and out of their flight,
watching it all,
unperturbed by the ending of things.
The space where they disappear
is the same green carpet.

The terrace blurs with sea foam blown in by the wind.
A cautious sun sweeps up the leaves
while in the seaside restaurant
a plate on the table imitates the solar disk
and already words meet up
in the warmth of summers to come.
Daylight timidly dabbling its feet in winter's wide stream.

The storm is close.
On shop windows the beautiful letters slant and disappear.
    Down in the riverbed
someone is hammering out
tomorrow's stone icon —
a hurried cheep cheep
to interrupt the lightning.
Soon we will see the shape of loveliness
twist its long fingers
across the plaited leaves of eucalypts.

4

Coming to the point where the window shines
not from any sun outside
but from the inner resources
of its memory of light,
such cold and powerful glowing,
and the woman
seated at the desk with herself as guide
continues with the quiet script.
In all the town the houselights are off;
shreds of toast
lie as offerings to the rats;
she sits within the music she writes.
The taste of emptiness, of dread
occupying almost all of her thin body,
her hand writes, detached,
and she offers
the notes of this oratorio that will be sung by no choir
to the forces that surround her,
invisible, menacing,
till the last voice goes out
and all around
the night sky slowly,
patiently
begins raining.

PAM BROWN

Writing poems is one of the things to do in these high-density, activity-laden, entertainment and information-packed times ... 'we no longer have roots, we have aerials' said the French guy ... it's not as if this world *needs* poetry.

A benign compulsion nudges my process. I track lines of thought. I use snatches and atoms of language and try to place them at some kind of slight slant to a linear norm. I collect & record glimpses. I aim for intelligibility.

To explain my method I'll quote from a 1997 poem 'Twitching'

> 'interstitial thinking —
> everything's
> a particle.'

To explain my attitude — When I read this stanza in 'The Regrets', written four hundred and forty years ago, it seemed Joachim du Bellay had summed things up for me ...

> 'Now I forgive the delicious lunacy
> Which made me use up all my best years
> Without my work bringing any advantage other
> Than the pleasure of a long delinquency.'

As for the new millennium, I can only wish, as I say in a poem called 'Prospects'

> 'to page-down this century
> as did, once, R Mutt.'

PAM BROWN

Abstract Happiness

50's values return
   the vinyl bunting fades,
      sunset's
   a bankable moment
         & a man becomes tearful
under an aerial photo
      of the city   he loved.
Indoor fingertips singed —
      stuck to a frosty tin
            of low alcohol beer.
   The wide din
of the take-off
   takes over   & you feel
like a decoy
      a clay duck
            a tin rabbit.

               O eastern summer
time   icy-pole paper
   blows in on a southerly —
         wind-sick
   & suffering
      shocking dreams:
pinned flat
      by a bus,
   hairy-faced women
cowering
      in ancient fear
            of the chloroform
                  murderer,
   the second bombing,
   a theme park crisis
      the carnival-tour-de-lex.

Recondite
   & difficult
      you supplicate
   via failure —
            it's only a tiny part

68

of the plan —
refusing to be shoved
  into virtue
    by ambitious hooligans
waving their dividends
        like paper flags.

Overcome, ultimately
    by museum-allergy
        (you've
  never liked the way
    a white straw hat
  says
   'english department'
    or 'film producer')
       you go for a walk —
Europe & Asia
  are over your head,
    in fact
from here   everywhere
    except Antarctica
is elsewhere,
    even in your home-town
  you'll need a map.

    ***

A feverish bee
  alights
    on your cigarette,
      a Salem,
& regards
  the bubbles
  in the lemonade.
How can you
  concentrate on
  the New Formalists
with the case-moths
    a-chomping
  through the ground covers ?

Where's the pesticide ?

Someone arrives
  with a book
   full of doozies —

(I've had
  a bookful
    of this !)

That Freddy Sauser
   is really
     Blaise Cendrars !
 & that ... that ...
Wilhelm Apollinaris Kostrowitsky !
    no connection with
      New Formalism
at all
 & BOTH
    patriotic zealots !

Now now   (bordering on
   critical)
     settle down !

Get Densey Cline !
  Quick !   Spray
    that wasp !
&   don't take
   the drooping balsam
     personally —

A volcano erupts   & you're caught
    pottering
      in the car-port.

       ***

Out of the rubble
   february follows february

The salvaged piano —
  a baby grand
  played by a grand baby,
       baby
(old hipsters smiling)

O lovely pleonasm :
  a tiny little child
        musician

Delicate as a daisy
   (I suppose)

& a tiny little sister
            singer,
        pretty as a peony,
   preparing twinkling scales
in the shade
        of a sequoia,
     entered, as if by fiat,
        in an eisteddfod

'What's
    a peony ?'
the little ones
         enquire.

            ***

Nothing stirs
      except a vague
           peripheral
      temple headache

& a half-emerged
      cicada
        killed off
by frantic ants.

This week's agenda —
    an interest
      in distant places —

Europe, Asia,
    Antarctica —
        shining loci
    for a hobby.

Blip

A b&w interview
exposes
a mouthful
of shining amalgam
about to indulge
in an outpouring —
to combat
this mild distraction
change channel
& find that
happiness is
to be so
artificial
as to double
as a biomorph
in a spot
where
three thousand things
a minute
take
place.

JOANNE BURNS

Between the late seventies and the early nineties I mainly wrote
prose poems — apart from a few fairly playful list poems of
which 'revisionism' is an example. I had rejected what I felt
was the restriction of the poetic line, and its knotted effect on
my poetry, for the looser, seemingly more casual flow of the
prose poem. I considered myself throughout all those years a
prose poet 'forever'. However in the early nineties, feeling a
need for more spring, tension, and shape in my writing I began
to write line break poetry again — but with what I felt was a
new prosy breeziness. This return to the more conventional
form of line break poetry was quite a surprise to me — a shift
in poetic identity. The prose poem is a fairly marginalised form
and it was easy to feel an outsider — a stateless person lacking
a viable passport in the putative world of literature/writing.
My prose poem writing retreated into the background.
However about a year ago I began to feel 'the line' was tighten-
ing up on me once again. So I again refreshed myself in the
wide open spaces of prose poem writing. Today I'm writing in
both forms simultaneously, and feeling that anything's possible
(even if it isn't). I'm becoming increasingly attracted to what I
call 'scatter' poems, with words scattered in small units across
the page, and I'm being drawn to the disjunctive and the
surreal — though absurd is perhaps a more precise term. You
need to give your words a good airing and shake up/out from
time to time. The more you write the easier it is to get bored
with your work, your poetic voice, and it echoes back at you
from the page like a cranky galah.

basket ware: a soft sonnet

when 35,000 write in for factsheets on how to stiffen
bows you know the nation's in need of urgent information
you can't just salve the population with ticker tape
parades our citizens are crying out for durable and pretty
decoration so why not let nature make a little contribution
to the scene: braid dried beaded ropes of seaweed into covers
for your tangled cords and plugs, fill festive baskets with teensy,
teensy pine cones to brighten your computer's hearth, dishes
of potpourri on beds of wood shavings should snuggle round those
pentium chips, yes a terrarium of african violets, a gulch of
assorted cacti would look welcoming on the cyberkerbs of
super-highways, and why not keep that conch shell handy when you go
surfing on the net: a tisket a tasket here comes aunt cleo
with her rustic infobasket, your tv's latest home decorator queen

revisionism

king lear in a mr whippy van
ulysses in a greyhound bus
heathcliff in a honda
miss havisham waiting for the lights to change

henry lawson in a holden commodore
silas marner in a mercedes
gertrude stein as a taxi driver
jane austen in a panel van

tennyson in a toyota
emily dickinson in a cadillac
voss in a campervan
hamlet in a valiant

huck finn in a volvo
lady macbeth as a removalist
the man from snowy river in a rolls
sartre as a petrol tanker driver

dickens in a mini moke
lawrence in a jaguar
hardy as a hearse driver
whitman in a four wheel drive

sylvia plath as an ambulance driver
eliot as a chauffeur
evelyn waugh as a rickshaw driver
proust with a flat tyre

together

in his tight clothes he walks down the hill like he's about to
inherit the world. in his tight clothes glued so fast to his body
you can see every movement of this walking x ray. life to him is a
series of parades. gotta be seen to be real. today is so cold yet all
he wears are jeans his girlfriend hanging round his waist and a
black t shirt whose arms have been carefully hacked out to show
us what he's on about. on its back is written THE STRUTTER. it
must be an emergency.

at the bus stop he and his girl hang snug in a barber shop
entrance near enough to be seen it's a public place the world. the
barber comes out and asks them if he can remove the empty can
of coke they have put on his step. they are too occupied with the
mechanics of kissing to reply. the strutter has his lips on her lips
and his hands on her hips. only just. he does not seem to want to
really touch in case something of himself would be lost in real
contact. they are touching yet they seem to be one inch apart.
he keeps gently pushing her back with his eyes moving to her
right towards an invisible audience he imagines then to the left
giving her glances of casual tenderness. between the thickness of

his hair his brown eyes glow knowing and furtive as foxes and his
long nose curves down into a wide mouth which has learnt how
to pout in innocence, which has learnt how to curl into hints of
menace.

they rock gently back and forth from each other on the
heels of their high boots. the bus is late and he is bored and
starts to pull things from his pockets to entertain themselves. to
show her who he is. there's plenty in his pockets. all are thin
items which slip neatly inside his waist like he has slits in his skin.
he opens a small key wallet and proceeds to place each of the
keys between the fingers of his right hand. he holds up his fist
which has become a weapon of five fingers of rough and savage
metal. he holds up his fist to her grinning like a child who has
discovered a rattle. he whips his hand down through the air
right in front of her face. the keys' points avoid her flesh by two
inches. after all he wants to be cool. but his eyes glint in the
expectation of the game of damage. she looks at him in a vague
sort of way. at the disco she tells her friends they're in love.

stereo

(from 'brief lendings: an architecture')

it puzzles you. the way these rooms bear so little
resemblance to your memories of them. no posters of che
guevara covering mould on the walls. no psychedelic
candles dribbling over neglected marble mantelpieces. no
stereos playing janis joplin donovan way beyond the
dawn. no cigarettes marinating in the dregs of flagon
claret. in recent dreams these rooms transform, magnify,
multiply. they bear a restless opulence: furniture, fabrics,
architecture of regal desire, brocaded ambition. you
wander through their alterations, disoriented. up winding
mahogany, rose, sandalwood staircases, along the
balustrades, drifting down lustred corridors, looking
through glass bedroom chamber doors for some

explanation. and there they are. all silent. inarticulate.
asleep. old acquaintances, rooms of ex-best friends. sunk
into their huge beds of silk and swan's down. their faces
lethargic. slightly feverish. their limbs, their necks slung
over the brass edges. credit cards, vitamins, and aspro
clear scattered like loose change anywhere on the mildly
dusty floor.

lumps

(from 'brief lendings: an architecture')

there's nothing substantial to unnerve you as you exit
from the lift at the basement level dragging your bags of
rubbish to the back entrance, to the bins. nothing but the
silence, the absence of lighting, the water that rolls
underneath the lift as it shudders back into motion. this
is the space of shadows, sitting underneath, listening to
the lives of tenants who occupy the fifty small apartments
above. this is the basement with its lumpy lino flooring.
with the doors in its walls padlocked and grilled. you
never meet anyone bringing their rubbish down at the
same time. you can imagine more than you need to about
the interiors behind the locked doors. it's best to
concentrate on making sure the garbage doesn't burst
through the bag before you deposit it outside.

back inside the lift the mirror looks at you. the dark
stained wooden walls with names like mike scratched on
them almost divulge information, histories to you as the
doors close so vocally. it's a lift that could feature in a
murder movie. a detective fiction. there's a strong sweaty
smell under the neon light although it is still the middle of
winter. as the door opens at your home level three floors
above you realise it must only have been the gas man.
you smell him as he steps back into the lift. as you step
out you mumble the beginnings of hello. to yourself.

JOANNE BURNS

wandering

(from 'brief lendings: an architecture')

you like it best for its deliberate anonymity, its catalogue
decor: the floral beds, the mirrors, lamps, the empty
drawers and cupboards, the ensuite bathroom, the nearly
empty fridge. clean, neat, new. you feel like its first guest.
you close the door, put the oversized key ring on top of the
large tv, drop your luggage anywhere at all and sigh. a
long sigh. as if you are in a cartoon. you inspect the tea
bags, the coffee sachets, the electric jug, the tiny
containers of milk that you know will end up squirting all
over you shortly. such miniature provisions. you unpack
your essential items: clothes, toiletries. this less than one
per cent of your total belongings. your small luggage bag
has never seemed so sufficient. almost perhaps excessive.
you lie down on the bed to fiddle with the radio, its
unfamiliar voices entering the silence like the unwrapping
of bright cellophane. you wonder what insights you may
have in this accommodation, this climate of domestic
absence. you are aware you could suddenly panic at the
possibility of feeling marooned, set adrift in indifferent
territory. so you get up, fill in the breakfast menu, turn
on the tv without sound, lie back and let your eyes wander

hygiene

(from 'brief lendings: an architecture')

to be middle class, fifty and a tenant in australia is
unpatriotic. socially embarrassing to all. like not
showering daily. washing the hands after going to the
toilet. corporate criminals, white collar conspirators doing
time in prisons manage to hold onto their homes.

78

CAROLINE CADDY

My last two books, *Antarctica* and *Working Temple* are, I feel, a culmination of the style explored and worked toward in earlier books.

The style evolved for a few reasons. One, my dissatisfaction with the carriage return effect, with little or no contribution to the poem itself, of left justified lines. Two, my self-perceived inability to read my poems aloud in public. As the style emerged I found it was my voice. Three, as well as phrasing and breathing, position on the page can give emotional or positive/negative inflections much as the position and colour of shapes on canvas. I wanted to be able to make more use of these effects.

Now I am having trouble with the words themselves, probably from having taken up the study of the Chinese language. Although the characters are not word pictures, the intrinsic relationship of Chinese painting and writing have left me dissatisfied with Roman alphabetic process.

As the song says, I am now looking at words like 'a one-eyed cat at a fish shop window', frustrated but keen to find another way in through the glass of over-familiarity.

It has thrust me back, as can be seen by the title poem of my next book *Editing the Moon*, to the wonderfully tactile sensations of pencil, paper and eraser.

Pelican

Aloof   long nose conjurer
impeccably out of style   watch him
he will show you the neat trick
of eating.

Dip and glide   another fish pocketed
in the deep box of his bill.
He lifts extendable wings
they are empty.

He points with a cold eye
summons his mate.   They preen
practise sawing each other
in half.

Snow

They look harmless –
                    gauzy torn wafers
                            that lift like flies
settle like ash.
I'm fascinated as if I'd lived all my life
            where even though it rained
                        it was a desert
                        without snow.
My shoulders grow soft epaulettes.
It feels like shelter.
Open the door and it follows
                    like a wraith of mosquitoes.
Fragile as green prickling a dark field
                    but it doesn't need green
getting on with some other
existence
    these stray flakes my imaginings
                        of what snow should be

while further out
the mass of its fall goes on
                    steadily building
                            with what looks like
being emptied.

Ice

Silently unfurling from seeds of cold
                        sepals sheaths labella –
tints and inks of ice
            twisting out of every slot and alveoli
                                ultra-blue
wave-length
            our eyes grow huge and faceted to see.
This is a white arboretum
of swollen roots and leaves –
                fungal rostrums
                        stuck at all the wrong
- or as dreams glue improbable veracities -
                            right angles.
We explore the ears of an embryo
                    the ocean grows
                            the sun melts
slewing rosettes and chevrons.
All day we push open
                shogi screens
                        with the tintinnabulation
of a frozen garden
and the long drawl of flowers
                        dilating
                            summer nights.

Huskies

If Einstein had a chance
to rethink his calculations
                I'm sure he'd put dog
                            as constant
from pole to pole
all through the runty screw-tailed tropics
                            that whiskery punch
that knotted rubber band of
            come in everybody's welcome
                        and stop right there
the same in any pack.
At the dog-lines they see us coming —
                get up from their palettes
                        of frozen urine
rumps high shoulders low   jaws fully expanded
then bounce and trample
                flexing thick backs
                    wagging the world.
They are indivisibly dog
inhaling each other's graven laws
            gnawing frozen protein blocks
                        into carcass.
It's said they can sense danger ...
                die thrusting
                    steadfast fallibility
into our harness.
We bend our tall hot musk to them
                    - our faces that are all nose
bare warm skin -
some more fraternal
            like that handler
                    with the wild red beard
who says he'll miss them —
            on their way to a better dog's life
                    pungent with trees.

Icebergs

Why do I think of sleep when I see them
                              rising angular above
their frill of slow waves?
Such width and steepness in anything else
would be dark inside —
                    but these have light in them
                              like a closed eye.
They seem utterly still — ... the way we want
                              sleep to be
but are full
of the creakings of hinge and interface
                              like a ship's
                              invisible flex
and astounding as sleep
when they shudder
                    drop their sides and we can see
                              into deep
turquoise energies.
I feel you turning in your sleep
                    like ice
                    with its mighty keel dissolved
up-ending slow as yawn
                    disgorging lumps
                              of indigo and black
wrestling your ocean
that rears and crawls
          subsides into dream
                    like beautifully warped sails
three or four coming together
and parting
pressing out blue from every lid and crevice
                              bright and stabbing
as the sheen
of live bone.
I stare at huge weathered torsos
                    jawlines
                              vivid and rivetting.
Here and almost freezing to death
                    step outside   observe
                              sleep.

83

ALISON CLARK

I see poetry as outcome of an urge to understand and feel my way into my experience as fully as possible. But why I have this urge and why it chooses poetry to express itself I don't know.

Being And Existing

You take your disquiet to lunch
in another suburb, the weather
meeting you more than halfway.
An impersonal wind batters
on the harbour. The white sky
turns hot and cold, quick change.

Not only is this not your territory —
you find you've drawn a supporting role
which requires nothing but your presence.
Is this asking too little or too much?
Pondering the matter leaves you speechless —
you could be cloud or island, but for the headache.

Yet how you long to be transparent: to be
and be seen to be, as sandy shallows —
no more personality like a cover,
the world thinking: Whodunnit, really?
But what means most to you
matters not to the world!

The Unhealthy Mists Of Lammermoor

See the dark lawn, the dappled light
and brooding trees. And see how the mind
full of anxieties is full of itself!
You could spend a lifetime like that —
making notes on the environment on the way
to something else, with the barren *pok pok*
of practice shots at tennis. Never quite
inhabiting your life, like a tenor
who can't act — fixed to the spot
amid the blood and tears, sword sticking out!

85

Pathetic Fallacy

One self goes to the country
hoping to hear from Nature.
The others tag along muttering:
You shouldn't have come!

A hard cold wind blows
its indifference over our heroine.
She is a ghost in someone
else's house, seeking herself.

The tangle of vine at the window,
the cane chair's weave left-to-right
as print, the ticking-striped wallpaper
which insists she read between the lines —

nothing! Like those old country walks
trying to hear the Word in trees,
night skies and water, as if Nature
were the voice speaking us;

or taking home the loops of magnetic tape
which drift about city streets
and playing them to hear meaningful words —
so strange, it might happen!

Delusion

The gods need handmaids, and handmaids need
to be of service. Loved by a god —
Woompf! Taken up as a jet of flame
to shine with reflected light in brilliant
folie à deux, beyond the loneliness of thought.

But then the gods must go (they have so
many dependents) about their business.
Colour drains out of the day.
Bereft maids eat disconsolately,
trying to staunch the sudden void

which opens between gut and diaphragm —
hunger for an expressible truth
between the is and is-not *nuancé* at the start
of a season's turning, or the moment at dawn
when light's presence is still debatable.

Tantalus

His urge to devour the world
makes it impossible to rest: he might
fix on one thing and miss the next.

The slow palpable life occurs to others.
Even the family's grainy banality and pains
acquire an aura of the ungraspable

to him — witness, phenomenally
attuned to reading lives for signs,
his mind a tongue in an oyster,

probing the original for its
mercifully obscure routines
as dumbly there as animals.

As in the neglected fairy's curse
or medieval vice or Freudian complex
his heart is always somewhere else.

Wherever he is,
beyond him lies the oasis where
everything is gleaming with itself.

Love will not help, nor sex the comforter;
once upon a time he was born, and from
that moment the world was not enough.

The God From Hyde Park

He has stepped from his plinth
between the mythological beasts and real ducks
and gracefully he lives among us —
seems to live: works, walks, eats, sleeps —
but love is harder for a bronze heart.

He, with an artist's eye for forms,
fondly inclines to this and that one;
but humans pursue a goal
which puzzles him: he'd like
his love to be not shared but seen.

Keenly he contemplates the body's
gestures, hesitations: to try
to read sex, mood and character therein
calls up his own — yet makes him
feel that he inhabits them.

Naked, muscular, serene, the youth looks back,
the huntress aims — larger than life,
forever acting what they're doing
for obscure couples traipsing past.
The ibis perched on a bronze turtle blinks.

ALISON CROGGON

I am interested, like all poets, in the relationship between language, consciousness and the body. This has been focussed by my work in theatre, where this relationship is literally dramatised. I attempt to create a quality of tension between raw emotional immediacy and a formal poetic aesthetic that has some affinities with Brecht's theory of estrangement. I am entirely unsure what kinds of poetry I will write in the future. Poets who are important to me include: Ezra Pound, George Herbert, David Jones, Pablo Neruda, Sylvia Plath, Rainer Maria Rilke, Sappho, Yves Bonnefoy, Anna Akhmatova, Catullus, Jaan Kaplinski, T S Eliot, Frank O'Hara, Derek Rukeyser, Paul Celan, H D, Geoffrey Hill, Ted Hughes, Hans Magnus Enzensberger (and so on). I prefer Swift to Pope, Coleridge to Wordsworth and Dostoevsky to Tolstoy.

Ode To Walt Whitman

Did you see me Walt Whitman beside my meagre river where I
        walk at sunset with my children
who whinge and buffet my arms and will not be led in any direction
marching with my sight closed to the rain and skittering seagulls
        while my children shouted look!
as the incandescent leaves shouted look! individual and numberless
        under the sodium light
although I hurried on nagging and impatient:
did you see me step off the sad trains in the hastening twilight
turning my face like a mint coin hope stamped on my mouth
to a night ambiguous with satellites
hearing in my secret heart the radio noise of murders half a suburb
        away
which all the loud news fails to report
Walt Whitman there are evenings when love withers inside me
the beat you thrummed with your syllabled fingers those joyous
        rebellious prosodies:
did you see the muscles of your teeming world
smashing the earth unstringing the massive harp of the sky
when you sang of your body returning alert as grass
or thrust out the spokes of your sight into the great unchanging
        wheels the miraculous sun and the tumultuous impersonal sea
Walt Whitman the gods are tarnished now the cities mourn their
        dead no longer
children roast in the fires of this terrible century
and no love is enough no elegy sufficient:
and yet I imagine you gentle imperfect generous man I would like
        to talk to you
perhaps you sit already at my shoulder whispering that nothing
        changes
that sunset is enough for its brilliance decay enough for its
        iridescence
old faker with your wise beard your lustful piety:
and truly what is my faith
except a stubborn voice
casting out its shining length to where I walk alone
sick and afraid and unable to accept defeat
singing as I was born to

The Elwood Organic Fruit and Vegetable Shop

I will go walking in Elwood with my mind as smooth as a marrow
winking at the unruffled sky throwing its light down for free
letting the gardens exude their well-groomed scents and thinking
        everything good
to the Elwood Organic Fruit and Vegetable Shop:
for the counter is democratically in the centre and everyone smiles
for people go on with the civil business of buying and selling
        under the handwritten notices
for bawling children are solaced with grapes and handled to leave
        no bruises
for the mangoes are soft yellow thighs and the strawberries are
        klaxons of sweetness
for the mignonette purses its frilly lips and snowpeas pout their
        discreet bellies and the melons hug their quirky shapes under
        their marvellous rings
for onions ringing their coppery globes and o the silver shallots
        and the hairy trumpets of leeks
for the cabbages folding crisp linens and the broccolis blooming
        in purple tulles and the dense green skirts of lettuces,
for peaches like breasts of angels and passionfruits hard and dark
        and bursting with seed in your palm
for the dull gold flesh of pontiacs and knotty umbers of yams and
        new potatoes like the heels of babies
for the tubs of sweet william and heart-lifting freesias and orchids
        damp and beautiful as clitoral kisses
for poignant basil and maiden-haired fennel and prim blue-lipped
        rosemary and o! irrepressible mint!
how they nestle up the vegetables, promising them the fragrance
        of their ardour!
the marriages which await them! the lips that moisten to meet
        them! glorious speech of the earth!

Songs Of A Quiet Woman

lurching delicate as a snow queen down this street of greys
unfocussed exactly enough to miss the businessman
goggling at my stockings   deciding
(as I twitch primly into my tram seat   my handbag
nestled on my lap like a puppy)   deciding
this will be a day of minor survivals:
etching a bloody mouth in fluorescent mirrors
or idly lacquering a hand of claws:
small weapons for a small war

*

there is one streetlight which always
blinks off whenever I walk near it
come home late and secretarial
to the hint of cats and cooking —
silently inside me something flexes
something unsurprised

*

men of course   lately they are kind to me
although an acid starting in my sweat
erodes me like an argument:
snatched by hesitation in a shop
eloquent and secret with the smell of him
I feel sureness swelling like a bruise
forcing blood into lips   breathless and reverent
this pearl in the corruption of my belief

*

(yes please no trouble thank you mother
it's been a pleasure because I do not know
how to be angry or ugly mother —
granny addled with sherry under bombs
in Winchester never raised her voice
or said a word back to your father
no matter what women or what insults:

her eighty year old skin is white and powdered
and now she pisses in the basin mother
and I know the proper way to lay tables)

*

to other things I turn the eye of god.
the tv's gorgon eye has glazed me over
and nothing touches me at all:
not famine fire fear or revolution.
only a twitching child in Beirut
firmly stroked to stillness by a nun:
he stared at her with eyes as black as hunger.
I wept then for the simple magic of hands

*

the routine of coffee   the complicity
of cigarettes and gossip
this gentle leaning over narrow tables
into the sly glass of recognition:
I know I am dishonest in my dress
(she says to me)   I know I am dishonest
but all I ever knew was how to lie

Prayer

Uncertain woman:
tomorrow the ducks
will flare and dissolve in the river's vortices
and the bridge will shudder again
under the weight of trains
and your hand will inscribe a page
pungent with futility, the barrenness
the blood brings you, the origin
its absence also grants you.

*

The children are asleep. One train
and the various roars of cars
and the fridge's ragged chugging
comprise my silence.
I think of you
and how only yesterday you kissed the skin
inside my wrist, the blue private skin
where my blood runs closest to the air.

Limbo

I am waiting
for what emerges
from the white edges
of catastrophe

that last bleeding note

bearing
this fragment
in my body
is a joy
beyond the dark
strength of my heart

and yet I choose
this labour

harder
every time

M T C CRONIN

I write poetry because for me it is a way of 'being' in the world. There are numerous purposes it serves — self-expression; communication with others; making sense of things confusing and bewildering; providing relaxation, stimulation and enjoyment; facilitating understanding of the world in both myself and others — but there are a myriad of things I could do to satisfy these needs. So why literature and why poetry? Poems, I think, are perhaps less open to (any and every) interpretation than many art forms, for example dance or painting or music, and probably more so than prose. They lie somewhere in a middle ground where the medium is incredibly pointed and complex and yet the author has chosen to say something in a less 'straightforward' way than normal modes of narrative or storytelling. Poetry is also a more concentrated and convoluted way of 'expressing' (which for me is 'living') what it means to be a self-conscious/self-aware human, than say the ordinary day-to-day activities that we all engage in and which are part of being socially alive — such as talking, touching, working, loving... All of this means for me that poetry is in some way an interaction of what is instinctive and intuited and not fully understood — the essential mystery — of humanness, with all that I am capable of as an intellectual and emotional entity who desires to 'make' ever more meaningful and wondrous images to push out into the conversation of life. It is a constant and yet everchanging joining of what I do not know and what I do; a way to learn how to be whilst immersing myself fully in being at the same time. (And I have great fun doing it!)

M T C CRONIN

Gnats On The River Nile

From our boat I see a bathtub
Sitting in the middle of the red clay
Women bent over it have mud between their toes
Their backs turned to us forever
I say I will take a photograph
Back to my friends' bathrooms
And say look at these prehistoric people
Isolated on islands living on orchid juice
Gracile bathing on the focused shores

But a gnat pushes through the air
And belts my cheek just before I
My camera is suddenly deep behind the boat
And I can no longer see the bathers
Those flies make river blindness says our guide

Dirty Foreign Laundry Policy

They fired a missile
In the middle of the night.
There was a tissue
In the wash. It's all over
Everything. The blood

Currimundi Beach — Eulogy

Back
from the zigzagging edge of the ocean

stands a red gum, alone, like a young flame.
there had been others…

now the dunes are full of young girls' bones
and they are trying to stop them blowing away;

the sea is no longer found in the sound
of rustling trees, the bush all cleared

fifteen years ago.
the gullies are hot

and full of brick veneer; young men in yards
beat tied dogs and fix cars —

the place is eighty per cent fences and the rest
kerbs: "nothin' to think about"

except chance and ignorance and social security
I'm back from the city

once every three years or so
out of compulsion, necessity, Christmas?

and head straight to the beach
we were the first people to move here;

put our house on a truck
and took it out of town.

set it down at the end of a sandy road
and walked the dog along the water:

too dangerous to swim, rips pulling
our suspicions the length of the beach

and back
it really was beautiful…

I grew up here
and I wasn't raped

(though as my sister says, "we may
as well have been…

all those bastards") and it doesn't seem
fun when I remember back

just frenzied and lazy and sad
drinking on the night strand;

boys' gritty fingers
and on the television's paranoid screen

a man dangling a noose from a car window
as his daughter rots in the sand

every day he returns there, grief stranded
and his tears are mythic

beached shellfish squeezing out salt water
every few years I return here, my father

picks me up at the airport
but there are no more shells on the sand.

He asks if I'll move back
and I say, I'm here for four days

The Confetti Stone

The black opal flecked with pink and green and the pale
buff-yellow of the tired wattle pressed into a damping earth

black and soft like nights when there are stars but you miss
them all, small silver pressed into the tasteless pudding

of the sky.

She kept the stone as a talisman against fear and rain
sounding beyond the window like cats' mouths chewing —

slip slip / slip slip of their wet pink gums
around something soft and bloody and dying.

In the palm of her hand it smooths itself to the size of an eye
or a far-off moon and casts enough light into the darkness of time

to light up the iron-bark standing lit like a city in the space
beyond the dam where just this morning away from the homestead

and garden she was confronted by a startled snake which had kicked
at her leg like a soft leather shoe, the acid-tape of its tongue

sticking fear to the roof of her mouth; but it didn't bite
just slithered over the grass that lay brown and shamed

by the persistent sun heating her face to the blush of roses
her mother had planted down the side of the house

where they tore at your skin in private.

He was dead now, her father, but once had mined this gem
under her fingers from land as hard as his thighs outstretched

like rods divining for the weakness in others; once
he had been a farmer... Now her family make money

from building and in the paddock her uncles erect the big tent,
striped in blue and white like a giant beach ball or hot-air

balloon or wet under the rain like a lolly licked by the canvassing
tongue of a child. Someone — a girlfriend maybe

or her mother — had tried to convince her to have the opal set
in a ring: like a memory in pride of place; like a black eye mounted

on the back of her hand watching her from the withered years,
crawled from its grave in the soil to watch her

as her father had done... And he didn't just watch but touched
with his prospecting fingers the body she will marry tomorrow

under the marquee to another man.

Tonight she celebrates her own wedding: marries
what she remembers with what she forgets, waits

with the stone heavy in her palm as outside the colours of the day
fight through black and break; where the dogs are barking

at a few old cows and the morning laughs reckless
in the thin-spread dew. She thinks of the drive down:

by the side of the road the not so occasional roos, bodies silhouetted
in humps by the suicidal light jumping in front of the car

and into the darkness and every minute of the way not wanting
to see the old house or the dam or the iron-bark or snakes

vanishing like death in the too hot days like her father heading off
with his small pick and shovel to the forgotten end of the farm.

And now she takes the confetti stone — sparks, rock-pink and grass
and wheat-field gold, buried deep in its sable shine — puts it in her mouth

and swallows him whole.

She'll marry her man on no sleep with a smile as wide as a barbed
wire fence; with her doubts buried deep in the creek's gravel

bed, in a dress stone-white and sullied by the paws of the dog they tied
with a crimson ribbon worrying its neck and drooping like the kids

at the end of the night. And she'll eat the aunties' cake they baked
and served on soft paper plates that lie around afterwards

as if the forgotten moons of a greedy planet and when it's all over,
all over, they'll drive away from this place unseen by snakes

or ghosts too busy to look up from sifting pans and while her
husband talks about cricket and rubs his thumb bent by the ball

all the way back to his wrist, she'll count telegraph poles
and fossick for opals in her head, not search the countryside

for a familiar stride under wide hat and shoulders while empty
of clouds, blue and captured, flashes by, the sky in the window,

a box of sapphire.

SARAH DAY

The poems I am preferring to write at the moment are discursive, starting with a germinal idea and drawing on imagery which is sometimes fragmentary and disparate and sometimes cohesive in the spatial development of this idea. These poems aim for detachment — I don't want the author's personal presence. Clarity of language and integrity of line are essential. My ear is always conscious of cadence, the sounds of words, independently and in combination, as I write.

Antigravity

Water surface cracks like cleaved granite.
A gull bolts through the fissure and enters the sea.

There is little time for the crab to reflect
on the elemental transition.

Its legs flail — a weak gesture of exultation
in air, antigravity that turns to SOS

in muddled semaphore and grows less comprehensible
as meaning, order are plucked away

like twisted, tweaked-off legs.
Between the wash and sweep of one wave

and the next, vacancy is complete.
A carapace with a hole the shape of a love-heart

dries beside a discarded claw
in a brief sketch of chaos in the sand.

Poxy Life

Feral Spitfires, cages were anathema
and they took them on, rightly so.
Fury alone ought to have made light of those bars;
siblings puzzled on the step in the sun
trying out the absence of the others,
the mother, ragged now from sharing herself
between them, sniffing the shadow of their panic
in the urine we'd washed from the shed floor
after they'd gone.
And then we scooped the lot. Packed off in two traps.
They broke the rules, simply by being alive,
were reasoned out of existence,

the tumbling and acrobatics
through the kitchen window, didn't work.
It was reasonable to cart them off,
to betray the sardines and artless sympathy.
There's no argument against doing the right thing
in a protestant country.
They should have been born in Rome
draping monuments and fountains,
where even the scabbed and blear-eyed
have kind words conferred,
can count on poxy life and tid-bits
ingenuously offered at dusk.

Deep Sleep

'The way of the slothful man is a hedge of thorns'
though the pricks stick easily enough
as I lie watching the sun dance on closed lids;
the fountain's chiaroscuro speckles my light thoughts,
immerses these green dreams in its deeps.
Bells ring in a week-day morning.
The world of work passes me by.

These gardens were a count's dominion once,
he's good enough to share them nowadays;
make yourself at home, please,
take in the knot garden at your ease.
Forgive me if I drowse —
the gods of ancient Rome gathered sentry
to this sleep or sleeplessness.
A rich man with no money.
Sun and water play my senses like harp strings.
This is Eden.
Wander at your will,
peruse the palm avenues,
climb the eastern stairs beneath the rampant vine,
the pagoda's a delight, my noble pantheon,

a view that's fit for kings, you'll find,
excuse the washing on the stone.

'Slothfulness casteth into deep sleep
and an idle soul shall suffer hunger'.
How water quenches the soul.
Earnestness and workers pass me by —
a shadow in the great metropolis.
(Grazie, so generous) they miss the point,
truth, beauty, innocence,
the garden's bounteous, the rest is pandemonium.

Here's wealth — water running from the aqueduct
through millennia, pure as gold.
This could be the backdrop for allegory,
Sloth leading the round of vices.

The hunchback with his barrow
skewering trash — who's he?
and his mate, the swarthy simpleton,
rocking, rooted to some inner zest
that bursts as operatic tenor,
soars on some days' elevation
past the bell tower?

No, the singer's Adam
and I'm Calvin's devil tempting God's bounty
(Grazie Signor, the good Lord be with you).
In the shadows of the shining city
snake the likes of me, trusting in benevolence.
Why not? there's beauty all around.
Listen to that tenor, pure melody of unreason.
Ah, show me the idle soul who will hunger
under the golden bounty of a midsummer sun,
even as autumn's clouds gather behind the
    Apennines.

SARAH DAY

A Hunger To Be Less Serious

When the bell rings at the canal bridge
it's as if the signal for release has sounded,
as if the people in motor cars unconsciously hoped for this all along,

as if they find themselves dismissed.
Doors open along the line.
The clay bank is suddenly colourful.

Upon the ringing of the bell, zebra gates, black and orange, swing to meet;
as they do, the whole silver body of the bridge veers in slow motion.
A Lego fantasy, a perfect mechanism.

The bridge marks its full arc then pauses,
describing a route for the reckless, the thrill-seeking, the desperate.
They picture it through windscreens: the brief ascent, the plummeting.

Water-surface puckers with the quick current,
underneath, the grey deepens steeply;
its effect is sobering, satisfying.

When she comes into view, the tub meets all expectations:
an old canoe-stern, trailing her fledgling nose-up in the wake,
sailing sublimely past the crowd and the procession of deserted vehicles,

away, away into the horizon,
carrying on board a gleaming catch
of strayed dreams and wish-fulfilments.

Iris

A single tapered bud
candlewaxed tight,

storm-broken
prematurely,

awkward,
too short in the stem for grace,

exposed
on a desk in a drinking glass

among papers.
For two days, cautious, resolute,

inert. Then it loosens.
Just a little;

relaxes the spiral
enough to see mauve

through green.
On the fourth day

purple spills out everywhere.
The idea has unfolded.

LAURIE DUGGAN

Adventures in Paradise

for John Forbes, John Scott and Carl Harrison-Ford

Near the end of the thirty-first year of my life
I find myself a bundle of sweaty neurones
under an umbrella shade in the courtyard
of the old Sydney University Union building.
What do I reckon has got me here and how?
I make a start on this autobiography.

Firstly, being a baby in baby powder
listening to Haydn and being fed
by an implement I think was called a pusher.
My grandmother wouldn't let my mother
hold me up in the bath. Is this
psychology? I don't remember much else.

Photographs give a few important clues:
the pattern of my father's cardigan
when he stood holding me up on the gate
at Beaconsfield Parade, South Melbourne.
I must have been looking out straight
across the road to Port Phillip Bay.

Then I'm sitting in a fruit box in the yard
with a dog called Sandy whose bones
I used to share. The place was a guest house
owned by my grandmother. I talked before
I could walk. Crawled up the stairs.
A man called Len Lovell fell off the roof.

The famous jazz musician Johnny Sangster
was a bohemian who lived in a bungalow
out the back. Upstairs there was a gangster
— incognito — who later got shot on the pier
in broad daylight. His real name was Freddy
Harrison. He held me at the breakfast table.

A lady threw lollies into the yard from the flat
next door. In a photograph we had cracked lino
on the dining room table and floor
and a Metters Early Kooka. My grandmother
had the room with the balcony upstairs.
Mussel and seaweed smells came from the shore.

My parents moved to Clayton when I was four
(this sounds like a line out of twelve-bar blues).
Every few months a man would come in a truck
and give me a few shillings for the empty
booze bottles which Dad stacked behind the garage.
Grandpa got caught on the dunny by the dunnyman.

When we got there the street was all mud
deep enough to swallow a baby, too deep
for cars. But we didn't have a car anyway
until Dad bought a 1957 Holden, but then
they'd almost made the road and all the market
gardens had all gone and I was at school.

There was a bakery near the station and one day
when Dad was sheltering from the rain
on the way back from work, a kid inside
called him a sour faced old bastard.
It got pulled down, became a wedding
reception room, then a hairdressing salon.

The doctor lived on the main street until
he moved around the corner. He thought I was smart.
My grandmother didn't like Picasso — for her
the sole representative of 'Modern Art'. I wanted
to be a veterinary surgeon and fix up animals
and live on a farm like my uncle and aunt.

I went to Clayton South Primary School;
half the yard was covered in pine trees,
the other half was open for football and cricket.
The bodgies used to build houses out of
pine needles and go down there to smoke.
The milk got rancid in the morning sun.

On holidays I went with Mum and Dad
to Bairnsdale on the 'Gippslander' and caught
a bus up the Omeo highway. My uncle
and cousin drove up the back paddocks
in a 1928 Chev to fix the fences. Sometimes
we camped in a tent on the river bank.

A friend of my father's I used to call Uncle Pat
lived around Footscray and worked in the abattoirs.
He was thin from being in a concentration
camp. I caught a tram to the meatworks
and a man cut out a sheep's eye and stuck it
on a post. 'That's to see you don't get in trouble, Son.'

Another uncle worked in a recording studio
and my aunt had a program on the radio.
They got me to say a few things 'over the air'
and gave me a free ticket to the Tarax Happy Show.
I was in a play in kindergarten in a chorus
of policemen and solo as a kangaroo.

Mum read me Shakespeare's sonnets and Milton
before I could talk. I liked them
but I didn't like the poetry much at school.
I had to learn off something by John Masefield
about the sea that he wanted to sail a ship on,
heavily stressed. I thought all poets old and bald.

My fifth grade teacher thought the two best books
were the Bible and the *Pilgrim's Progress*
but I was more interested in the dinosaur
and fighter aircraft of the second world war.
I had a great uncle who copied out passages
from Tennyson on greeting cards in tiny writing.

Apart from that I didn't do very much.
I learned to ride a bike and went to high school
and got 27 for arithmetic in the second form.
I think I still wanted to be a Vet., though
cartography came next. I was in the Boy Scouts
and got wet sleeping under a picnic table.

I burst a blood vessel below the brain
and spent two months in the Alfred Hospital
reading the complete works of Ian Fleming
which I liked because he could make golf
interesting. Then I read Emile Zola
and started writing D.H. Lawrence imitations

in which young men full of spirit flung
themselves down on the earth and felt it breathe
and everything seemed complete. I wanted
to be a rock star, then a painter,
then a novelist, but I ended up writing poems
late in 1966, misunderstanding T.S. Eliot.

Next year I got into trouble for a satire
about Dame Zara Holt in the school magazine
that came out the week the Prime Minister
swam out to sea with his snorkel and wasn't seen
again. Australia was all the way with L.B.J.
and the girl I loved loved someone in the Labor Club.

I raged at Monash in check pants and a black
roll neck jumper. This was the age of 'progressive
rock'. Someone got into trouble for staging
a mock crucifixion outside the Union Caf.
The vice-chancellor sputtered about the disinterested
pursuit of knowledge. I stopped copying Keats

and started to copy William Carlos Williams:
the absurd sonnet turned into the stick poem.
Lots of grown up poets visited the university
and read to the Lit. Club, all pissed on flagon sherry.
Chris Wallace-Crabbe competed with billiards
near the billiard room and the billiards won.

Some of the other poetry was more fun,
like Robert King dancing to bongo drums
and ripping his shirt off, or when B.A. Breen
read concrete poems with repeated words and when
an old academic asked him his definition of verse
Rob Smyth chanted POETRY POETRY POETRY.

There were marbles under police horses' hooves
on the fourth of July, and Colin and Margaret
stared at candle flames while Iron Butterfly
played 'In-a-gadda-da-vida' and the doors
of perception opened wide. A weight ounce cost
twenty dollars. The 'underground' lived in Carlton.

Sometimes we'd drive in with boots of lager
to La Mama to hear some situationist verse.
I wrote a Dransfield parody: Acid Fuck Raga,
and got told off by Geoff Egglestone
for not taking *his* work seriously. It was bad
but the Melbourne Uni. poets were worse,

writing about martyrdom in Parkville
on mornings before lectures with the shakes;
imagining themselves as William Blakes.
Not long after this the combination of dope
and footnotes in the work of Alexander Pope
convinced me the era of the Stooge Effect had begun.

It was the dawning of the age of Aquarius.
I visited Sydney and wanted to stay there;
went to the Canberra Arts Festival with
a headband, two scarves, long hair, three sets
of beads and an army jacket and read to an audience
for the first time without going blind with fear.

Next year I moved to Sydney and a room
upstairs in Crown St., Surry Hills
with Pam Brown, poet, and an American groupie
with a waterbed and the bass player
from Led Zeppelin. Albie Thoms was shooting
funny movies about light from the front window.

Labor came into power. I missed the ballot box
and took a trip on a piece of blotting paper
thinking the party lights on trees in a Petersham park
had something to do with the advent of Socialism.
The blue V.W. spluttered through Glebe
bringing the pages of Zap Comix to life:

The me decade had begun. The age of subsidies,
safari suits, sonnet sequences, and the death of art.
The houses in the Glebe estate got repainted,
rents went up, people were psychoanalysed,
but all this seemed to happen very slowly.
I had a job in a public library

stamping out books, taking too many sick
days, moving out of too many houses
to return as a tourist and watch them stripped to brick.
Poetry too was beginning to wear its tweed
jacket again, and speak in muted tones
about the spiritually edifying architecture of Florence.

Briefly — I fell in and out of love
and in and out and in and out some more,
swore off drugs and took them up again,
finished two books and started on a third:
was granted a modest place on the honours list
whenever two other Sydney poets got together, pissed.

Blue Hills 24

Half an hour down a straight road
from the prison farm, Boof Morgan sings Country
to a synthesizer, a drum machine
and a dozen desultory lovers of genre.
A man and woman mime each number
while the barman lives by reflex
metres from where the boats tie up.
Thickset men with beards and cowboy hats
gather elsewhere, under the bar TV
They are no friends to this music
— wear its apparel with no concern
for a pickup draped with the national flag
— departed next day from this fine drizzle
across a map of blue skies and faithless love.

DIANE FAHEY

As my poetry has developed, it has led me towards the themes of ecology and storytelling. After writing a collection based on insects, *Mayflies in Amber*, I turned to sea creatures for inspiration, and have a work in progress on that subject, called *In Praise of Sea-Horses*. I would love to follow that, if it's given to me to do so, with a book on birds.

After two books based on figures in Greek mythology — *Metamorphoses* and *Listening to a Far Sea* — I'm now writing poems on Grimms' fairy tales for *The Sixth Swan*, which is near completion. After that, I'd like to explore the tales of Northern Europe, further selecting from Hans Christian Andersen, E T A Hoffmann and others. Ultimately, I would hope to find myself writing on Irish fairy tales.

Another book I'm now researching is a verse novel set on a train travelling from London to Edinburgh on the last evening of the nineteenth century. It will be called *The Mystery of Rosa Morland*, and a varied cast of characters is already assembled... I thought of writing this book because I love mystery stories and am increasingly fascinated by the Victorian period. Also, approaching as we are the end of this century, it seems natural to cast one's eyes back to the end of the previous century.

Because I'm deeply interested in the Gothic, I've written various poems on Dracula and Frankenstein, and would like to build these into a sequence called 'Modern Monsters' which would be the centrepiece of a more varied book of poems. I expect to write less directly personal poems from now on, but will continue to record my responses to natural settings, in particular those close to river and sea.

Snow

… sometimes he himself, who feared that if I lost track of him I should despair and die, left some mark to guide me. The snows descended on my head, and I saw the print of his huge step on the white plain.
— Frankenstein

Always, at the back of my eyes, I saw
my pursuer. An intemperate peak showed
wild gashes tracked by toothprints —
small clean bites of them, till they meshed
with a new rhythm, flailing towards chaos:
the death of a mind, its every device
and delusion an embellishment on snow.

At last, alone. Even in that unbounded place
I felt in myself a vastness, imagined
whale inside iceberg, as I staggered towards
sea-line, thirsting for a frozen magnificence,
to be preserved inside a tower that could
travel oceans, slice ships, buckle ice floes —
an island where no tern lands.

Teiresias

Drag queen (retired)
back in a suit and sober tie —
almost convincing

but for face-flesh sagging
under the memory of
too much make-up;

lashes burdened
at fluttering moments
by blue ghosts of mascara;

mouth a little too wrinkled
even for your wide
slipstream of years.

You re-entered woman
in the only way you could,
mimed her movements

till finally a birth into
this new/old self,
this serviceable enigma.

What to do but be
philosophical, though
it's difficult to rest

inside a body that knows
almost everything
about what it's not.

These days, you give advice
from unpursed lips,
point up plain truths

deviously/directly
— as is *de rigueur*
for prophets.

The envious and the curious
only pretend to believe
while they drink in

as if it were nectar
the atmosphere around you,
scan unseeing eyes for

signs — for swords of light
carving that shining
grey dusk like lasers…

When they go — sometimes,
this fusion, this dissolving,
as shadows slide back

beneath skin, and
all that you have lived,
you become.

Macaws

So this is what parrots become
when they let themselves go,
allow excess to roost in their souls —

breasts in sunglasses-strength saffron;
blue wings an untidy archive of
noon to first star; old-jewelry-box

tarnish on ragged wedding train…
Huddled in nit-picking love
they touch beak-coloured tongues;

drape swathes of plumage against
each other; in amplified propinquity,
air pinions touchy as radar.

Jesters more than saints, yet
at times a piercing probity,
the hint of immutable intentions

as heartbeats rock long-dead branches.
Near dusk, a royal progress from perch
to sequestered cage — mobile bric-a-brac

colonising a Victorian parlour
with shrieks that could wake the dead,
or scold them back to sleep:

this gorgeous waddling into the dark,
the light on their feathers undressed by it,
zebra-lidded eyes noting you,

the exotic, without condescension;
wisely adapted, fantastically sane,
lacking only a rainforest.

The Sixth Swan

The six shirts were finished, except for the one that still lacked its left sleeve ... The moment the shirts touched them, their swan skins fell off, and there stood her brothers, strong and handsome. Only the youngest lacked his left arm and had a swan's wing in place of it.
— The Six Swans

A waterfall of feathers spills from his left shoulder.
He's tempted to tilt his body sideways, limp,
convulse his features, but finds with practice
a measured stride, an expression — half-open,
half-closed — that will meet the situation.

Wealthy enough to hire a tailor of genius,
leisured enough to choose a life of letters,
he slides a brocaded cuff across vellum,
trailing feuilletons, odd gnomic poems:
monocles to quiz moonlight, seed unearthly fires.

Above sloped fingers, his quill embroiders air;
stops; moves resolutely on...He has picked up
the dropped stitch of his first lost life.
There will be lapses, eccentricities, of course.
For one, he frequents the highest tower to see

flocks pinwheel the sunset, fracture in storm
or swim through cloud-surf, breasting noon's topaz.
At such times his eyes become dangerous jewels
that fade to dulness when someone is sent to
guard him: 'My, but that spectacle is ravishing —'

(eyes subtly turned), 'they reach such heights!'
'Yes,' he rejoins wearily, 'it *is* a long way down.'
But he's not tempted. If he feels a tremor
of that winged life pass through him,
his whole body unnerved, displaced from itself,

as a great white shadow twitches and tingles —
athirst to be silvered by sunlight, to arrow
through cobalt space above miles of conifers —
well, that is all so much rhetoric…

                                        His wing
settles into his side like moulded parchment.

It is only having two arms again would break him.
And had he two wings it would sadden — he'd be
a homunculus-bird, a lard-wrapped angel…
He climbs the steps of the tower. It's midnight.
The sky is a page of stars he can't write on,
a compendium of invincible memories.

Awakening

From the tilted jug, water began to flow
so that the page could slake his long-held thirst,
the cook sluice onion-grief from her eyes
then slice the trout kept moistly gleaming
in time's aspic. At last, the kettle boiled.

As if to upstage a century of silence,
peacocks screamed theatrically against
emerald backdrops starred with violet on
midnight-blue on bronze ... all ferried with
disdain across the ordinariness of lawns.

The last of the steam rose from a hoof gripped
by the blacksmith's leg-of-mutton hand,
the instruments round the forge wobbly,
phantasmagoric, as the horse knew what
heat was again, and snorted as iron struck earth.

Instantly, the garden was recolonised
by larks and butterflies, blackbirds, wasps;
fresh seeds floated abroad. Gilt carp sent up
messages bubbling through silver-green:
Carpe diem...Water lilies sucked slime.

After her long moment of lese-majesty,
the queen contemplated, over multiple
chin-folds, the intricate lattice of honey
snarled in the lace of her puce velvet bodice,
a last filament looping from her crust-filled mouth.

Bent at an uncomfortable angle floorwards,
the king picked the gold piece from the parquet —
alive, as never before, to its resonant chill,
so that his heart was a flower in early summer;
and — first checking the door was locked —

he smiled broadly around at all his bags full —
his precious children, most loyal subjects,
the twinkle-twinkles in his royal blue sky.
The peacocks' scratchy music drifted in as,
dreamily, he caressed the pain in his lower back.

In the topmost room of the highest tower,
the princess was recalling — hazily at first,
then sharply — that impulsive finger-prick.
Blue-green eyes opened upon a crimson tear
welling from a fingertip. She bound it with

a cloth of cherries embroidered on snow.
Her lips felt sea-changed: only now did they
know their softness...But her skin was chilled —
that presence blocking the light! When he bowed
and stepped back, she saw, like a question mark

above his head, that feathered spire; beneath,
aquamarine eyes looked back at her as if
her own. She stirred upwards, wanting to glimpse
the secret garden within the palace wall
and those far kingdoms crowding the window's map.

Between, a nightmare hedge of briars woven with
bony hands. She screamed! — would have it hewn down,
made a bonfire! Then, turning to her companion:
'Tea? — or perhaps wine?' He'd come a long way —
those princely garments torn, earth-stained.

Down they spiralled into the heart of the castle
with its hum and clatter. Time later to savour
new silences, plumb the mystery of bodies
flushed to boiling point, then slowly cooling
in an alchemy of sweat, a radiance of propinquity.

LIONEL FOGARTY

Murra Murra Gulandanilli
Waterhen

Yet I too bleed the Murra Murra Gulandanilli heart
We blessed his body touched
We slipped to the earth feel with Daniel
I stepped proud, yielded dance
That was denial
My radical grumble with him
Oh man oh man
Him smiling at you,
Him a-laughing at you
Him eyes are dillil
Him understood the street lies
Him undertook eight and was mistook
Murra Murra Gulandanilli
Pain and ache
Yet he was loved by the Great Ones
Grief came out, out of sharing
And sharing and sharing alike was him
I still to this day feel
Danny Yock's consistency
The fate him kept
Paradise him kept
Dayock is a-calling contempt
To evil policies
Dayock is a-singing to the souls
Aborigine revolution coming
To those pigs sneer and judges too
Dayock want all you young to fight on
Not lurk on
To fight on To defend him
Dayock fear nobody
Cos him was a spiritual dancer
Was a Murra Murra dancer
Everybody praise within his respects
A distant happier came for a far a-wide
A-wide

Just a-greet Danny Yock
I asked a light of life and people
Here to 'member
The ember of the human spirit
To make him our brother Daniel dance that dance
Of the bleeding Murra Murra heart
He was taken away, taken away from me
in my heart living in always
The journey of his beginning
No more pain no more suffering
Dreamtime dancer keep me strong
Murra Murra Gulandanilli
Culture romancer
You're on the other side, the light you see
The light you see is where you're from
Is where you're going to be the from of the feeling that was
    within you
Can't you forget
Can't you remember
As long as I am a-grieving
You'll see justice will be done
Baba Yubbu
I will love you always
Your blood runs through me
I'll survive, we'll sunrise the enemy
At Murra Murra Gulandanilli dancer
The culture romancer
In my heart you're living always
In a Murri way of dancing
Dreamtime dancers
Romancers dance
Murra Murra Gulandanilli
Waterhen Waterhen Waterhen

Biral Biral

Biral came down one day
crystal stones went where none would dare.
Just a little boy, known by everyone
send a flower picked for this one, time expressed
Reply had to be made, springs invoked
'Who is Biral?'
Walking alone sharp rocks cut my feet
leaf push upon my skin.
Bad tribes were known to never return
greatest healthful huge size spirit
enters manhood
taking violence away
fading in a day.
Morally, I'm not better off.

Nugunda supreme. Live spirally in my being.
Death inflicts existence
too real for this world.
Supernatural customs differ to human
now tribes who have lives on
fellow of the nameless kind.
Journeys, new born, mixture powder
a virility more wonderful than risks.
Magic escape compassion, no good to say.
Space veined howls around knowledge, bitter gift
the sucking bloodless fed strong men
feared in homeless whirl, by passwords.
Ambush admitted the tunnel of music
entered the little boy now known by everyone
Trumpeted the didgeridoos
operaed a stranger calls.
Speaking souls, race blows weird things onto faces
made u'fella look like creatures of another era.
Sweet simple bodies, paths shadows
dazzled masked ritual and religion.

She turned, asking her people
I've never seen Ngunda
So why show a boy meaning nothing
a little boy, smaller than an ant
looking for a fight with porky pines.
My answer shattered in storms.
and disposed in scrubs where none haunts
and where river parts inside my guts
for I am 'belief'.

Beauty, parents may protect helpless creeping country babies
but will they point the way to waterhole.
Mountains lazy survived future dispensed
cause land felt slaughter to any who lifeless the hills
Fish and snake rest, while people eat rope
they hung themselves.
Wicked terrific scenes came
diversity sensational, all down the tracks at night.
This relationship I previously had, shorter
now it longer
so however highest degree or what the spirit dwells
deep and contemporary in us
it is within
Watching morning asleep
but gunya, sparkling stars windowed at darkness
a giggle swept tears
winning a day and night
no a stomach tight and empty, crawling
search a prey over near grasses
shapes stretched to marvel
then dreaming forced Mum, Nanna and lotta people
shouting, me to sing out
Weakness no more
Ngunda
Biral
Many influences, many spirits
Nguthuru too.
These words, not vocation
Born, inbred by Aboriginal people
I'm blood. Sheer and delightful.

Disguised, not attitude

Distances run sport to a tested vessel
wander over teams, sailing with economics in mind.
Absorbed, unlawfully driving juvenile delinquency
they appeared.
Wrenching survival, peered bent engulfed dominances
inching advising, achieving came relieved into social skills
the pride fosters no interests in developed traditions.
Walks her texture of eternity
pedestals are matched cries in the winds.
Verandah rainbows shape, now mass rustling to shrieks
a star, relaxed when fell on this globe.
Purple sky during day smoke comics of life
highways prepared one way trips
this chimneyed all blacker
and still war, glorious, is always devastating
Young fit numbers where are records off
deprived by in-between tent-men.
Sheer encouragement can improve strokes
where corrugated iron can't brake it.
Confidence sprints near our semi-tribal tourists looks.
Anticipated potential inhabitants shook impelled stillness
transfixed, now the vine
courage ran out.
Liquid buried sprang voices
rawed opinions gutted by problems, public kept.
Review still in your education
said to struggle better?
Handout confluence mortgages instructed your asserted civil
Recite history piled together hesitationly
then wooden taboo won't case mistaken places
Yes, bushey's parks unexplicable to sight
even grassing lands remained tense.
Massacres rich earth paws and forces by coming
Aboriginal to this settler.
Chosen errors, stories blame grasp. Ah, Ah, Ah
centre forgiving (not by you hopefully)
Fried caught expectation licensees
swung beings to attractive attract.
Boast tongue moderation
cause venom academics a stir

just for felicity in scenery
are palmed blacker.
'Get lost', so is mine
Voluntary work, conservatives
you never make Murris
Misfortunes can't go out here or credited
seem to provide dispute, refute and surrender splendour.
Yet obeyed invaded forbears innocents are spiritual
and conflicting cultures titles one peace
and pure airing
than loyalties, thousands volunteer again
Wealth furthers millions, appalling
novelists tremendous, now trembles encompass enfolded faith
Praise brilliant Gilbert, mastered living blacker
cause renegade seeks in Kevin.
Writers bastard from overseas, a bare face lie
Now all books speak, land ecology never have holiday
when nuclear murderers
but ash writers test peered interests
not over us'fella
for again published musts are
'Long live Davis, Walker and Gilberts
writers
we yours'.

Jukambe Spirit — For the Lost

Jukambe
Don't we all have your spirit
Bleed sores between teeth
Feeding lighting rocks
My Jukambe will devote, come giant shelter.
My distant Jukambe host a tribe
I'm with your journey standing tall striped away
felt intervals for coastal Murris
are relation to Yoogum Yoogum.
How several mountains came
one loving brainy social wantness

Yea Jukambe fruit a result
But most of us live city private
our knowing each cone is lumped
killing important
My tribe were among white mans ownership
grouped they claimed on Jukambe tear
and distant areas
Roasted raw the bunya nut
unriped ceremonies
initiation coming over elaborated wide territories
now massed by houses and sales
my people nutritious a seed
and brings boils over their bodies
if they wanta get unsick
Nature, Jukambe might tell or lend.
Collectively my people now
I don't see at grassland or hill creek track
where Jukambe worked and played.
Yea my some communication, still many tribespeople
dialect young and old, not sold.
Yea, bunya pines brighten old Jukambe members Yoogum.
individual; to keep children Yoogum
The stories, bodies and mind, exact
cause hard telling all youse
Jukambe is my people, cause white mans name taken place
Relived, I am. In your spirit, Jukambe.

A Lie

Way out in the valleys and
mountain ranges of light

You came quiet in roaring tide
in the sunset lagoon
How softly whispers the river
and streams in endless waters
THOSE
can't tell a Lie.

JOHN FORBES

John Forbes died tragically in January 1998. He had approved the following selection of his poems but not yet written a statement, though he had intended to do so. This anthology is dedicated to his memory.

Stalin's Holidays

The quick brown fox jumps over the lazy dog.
Juniper berries bloom in the heat. My heart!
'Bottoms up, Comrade'. The nicotine-stained
fingers of our latest defector shake as they
reach for Sholokhov's *Lenin* — the veranda is
littered with copies — no, commies, the ones
in comics like 'Battle Action' or 'Sgt Fury
& His Howling Commandos'. Does form follow
function? Well, after lunch we hear a speech.
It's Stephen Fitzgerald back from 'Red' China.
Then, you hear a postie whistle. I hear without
understanding, two members of Wolverhampton
Wanderers pissed out of their brains, trying
to talk Russian. Try reading your telegram —
'mes vacances sont finies: Stalin'. But we don't
speak French or play soccer in Australia, our
vocabulary and games are lazier by far. Back
in the USSR, we don't know how lucky we are.

Love Poem

Spent tracer flecks Baghdad's
bright video game sky

as I curl up with the war
in lieu of you, whose letter

lets me know my poems show
how unhappy I can be. Perhaps.

But what they don't show, until
now, is how at ease I can be

with military technology: eg.
matching their *feu d'esprit* I classify

the sounds of the Iraqi AA — the
thump of the 85 mil, the throaty

chatter of the quad ZSU 23.
Our precision guided weapons

make the horizon flash & glow
but nothing I can do makes you

want me. Instead I watch the west
do what the west does best

& know, obscurely, as I go to bed
all this is being staged for me.

Death, an Ode

Death, you're more successful than America,
even if we don't choose to join you, we do.
I've just become aware of this conscription
where no one's marble doesn't come up;
no use carving your name on a tree, exchanging vows
or not treading on the cracks for luck
where there's no statistical anomalies at all
& you know not the day nor the hour, or even if you do
timor mortis conturbat me. No doubt we'd
think this in a plunging jet & the black box recorder
would note each individual, unavailing scream
but what gets me is how compulsory it is —
'he never was a joiner' they wrote on his tomb.
At least bingeing becomes heroic & I can see
why the Victorians
so loved drawn-out death-bed scenes:
huddled before our beautiful century, they knew
what first night nerves were all about.

133

Watching the Treasurer

I want to believe the beautiful lies
the past spreads out like a feast.

Television is full of them & inside
their beauty you can act: Paul Keating's

bottom lip trembles then recovers,
like the exchange rate under pressure

buoyed up as the words come out —
elegant apostle of necessity, meaning

what rich Americans want, his word is
like a poem, completing that utopia

no philosopher could argue with, where
what seems, is & what your words describe

you know exists, under a few millimetres
of invisible cosmetic, bathed

in a milky white fluorescent glow.

Ode to Karl Marx

Old father of the horrible bride whose
wedding cake has finally collapsed, you

spoke the truth that doesn't set us free —
it's like a lever made of words no one's

learnt to operate. So the machine it once
connected to just accelerates & each new

rap dance video's a perfect image of this,
bodies going faster and faster, still dancing

on the spot. At the moment tho' this set up
works for me, being paid to sit and write &

smoke, thumbing through Adorno like New Idea
on a cold working day in Ballarat, where

adult unemployment is 22% and all your grand
schemata of intricate cause and effect

work out like this: take a muscle car &
wire its accelerator to the floor, take out

the brakes, the gears the steering wheel
& let it rip. The dumbest tattooed hoon

— mortal diamond hanging round the Mall —
knows what happens next. It's fun unless

you're strapped inside the car. I'm not,
but the dummies they use for testing are.

post-colonial biscuit

vibrantly dead,
world of air-conditioned
absence (a girl comes in
once a week
to keep the green plants clean)
                    but is the smell of

flesh,
sweat
faeces
salt, bolts of bright cloth

JOHN FORBES

bells around stalls to keep the spirits off
                    in a carpark turned into a market
any more natural?
oh spring backed folder of my lust
you wear a helmet to bed
& wake up circling a dirt airfield
totally socked in (is the shriek of wind
in the taut wire rigging
or the fine mist of oil
on a perspex windscreen
any more natural, any less?)
a balanced head that dreams
like an old style lolly machine,
                    a talent to abuse
& a pair of secateurs are all you need —
                    that, & shade enough
to keep off the itch
of hot plastic on a humid day ...
fallen mangoes stain the concrete
around the drained swimming pool,

tropical flowers overwhelm their pots:
the rest you have
to sketch yourself
because this poem lacks form & structure,
isn't going anywhere in fact —
                    '& that',
an urbane, Third World
voice breaks in,
'that is your triumph, your triumph
& despair,
                    because you know
no weather
really stops
Hercules packed
with ex-pats
taking off
& while I miss the pipeband music
you used to say goodbye with
I love the biscuits in those
plastic ration pacs — they're great!'

136

PETER GOLDSWORTHY

Poetry is always deeply memorable utterance. Poems stick in the head the way music lyrics stick. This may be biological: a deeper structure of rhythm, rhyme, assonance and epigram (and music) may be hardwired into our brains to augment their faulty memories. Before writing, all knowledge had to be remembered in the form of poetry or song. Many Aboriginals still remember knowledge that way — the songs and poems of the Dreaming are an encyclopaedia.

I see jokes as a subspecies of poem. Their timing and rhythms and word order must be remembered and repeated perfectly. A good poem is no different: leave out a word, it's ruined.

Of course, poetry written according to these prescriptions can be too word-perfect, too finished. Coming from a background of minimalism and irony, I have been trying to loosen up my own poetry in recent years. Irony is a safe defence against committing what I like to call the fake orgasm in literature — the genre of the pretentious, and rhetorical — but it is also, finally, a limiting mode, and a negative mode. There is a ground-zero levelling in the refusal of minimalism to take real emotional, or even rhetorical, risks.

Jan Owen once told me that instead of trying to write each book better than the last, we should try to write worse. In other words, we must let go of taste and conscious override to some extent. Poetic experience is commonly regarded as something unmediated, purer, first-personed — something that comes from a little deeper in the throat than prose writing.

Poetry might also be the closest language can get to expressing the way we actually think — which is not in words only, but also in images, feelings, songs, sounds. That is, poetry might be the closest we can get to representing Mentalese, or Brainish (or whatever we might call the deep language we actually think in and with) within the confines of a verbal language.

Chemistry

1. Glass

Inside my father's shed
I notched and snapped
a hollow cane of glass.
Softened in a yellow flame
transparency became opaque:
a glowing, drooping stalk,
syrup at its golden tip.

I bent and stretched and blew
without inhaling once,
wasting many pipes
until the molten toffee cooled
and hardened into crystal
shapes, and I had breathed
an apparatus, a still of glass.

2. The Still

Ingredients were placed by measure
inside the blown globe at left-hand end,
like subjects in a sentence yet to come,
a glass machine whose moving parts
were heat and vapour, flowing left to right,
the way we think words on a page.

The cooling column
was a waist,
hollow narrows,
equals hinge
between two halves
of an equation.

Beyond this bottleneck
the sum or minus distillate squeezed out
in pure and simple form, the right-hand
side of declaration, arrived at

less by magic than by see-through logic:
a wand of glass, a method that worked.
Or didn't work for reasons that worked.

3. Water

It turned saltwater into fresh,
removing taste so utterly
that there was nothing,
not even tastelessness,
an absence only, like
the taste of water in the night
inside a mouth that's warm
and dry and still confused by sleep,
or like the taste of glass itself,
the zero flavour of the vessels
that we keep our water in,
that give our water shape.

Stand and cool, then add back
a pinch of salt for flavour.
I still prefer the drinking water
that we pipe into our homes,
that splashes, stereo,
from faucets when we twist
the volume knobs, that faintly
tastes of river mud and metal,
like the heavy water
that we mostly are ourselves
inside these baggy, greasy
waterproof wineskins,
impure and unclear.

4. Alcohol

I once thought booze
proof of God:
two carbon atoms
and two common gases,
fermentable from anything at hand.

Why should such simple stuff
work magic on the mind?
It seemed an obvious gift,
a rain that fell from heaven.
(The rain that falls in heaven.)

Clearer and colder than water,
its icy heat, all distillate, filled
my veins with pickling spirit,
drowned me from the inside out.

Surf's up, I said at school.
My drinking friends came round.

5. Bromine

Bromine is my favourite
element, period.
Its crimson fumes corrode the corks
and eat the rubber bungs
until the first red-purple drops
gather in the cooling column
like ruby grapes, unpressing
backwards out of wine,
in time-lapse, fast-reversed,

and falling into water
from the glassy neck
as heavy and uncrushable
as mercury, quickcrimson
and semi-solid, sealed safely,
unexplosively, beneath the surface
of the clearer lighter fluid.

6. Ether

The recipe for cooking ether
I've forgotten. One level tablespoon
of concentrated nitric acid

plus heaped teaspoonfuls
of poisonous powders, misc.
The names are gone;
from that short night
only this comes back:
drops of ether gathering
at the distal ice-cooled tip
like tears, like even clearer
moonshine, swelling till
detachment weight,
then falling, falling, gone;
vanished into dreamy vapour
before they hit the bench
under which I slept.

7. Acid

There is a big name acid,
hydrofluoric, which eats glass.
For my last trick I distilled
that high and mighty octane,
standing just outside the shed,
in safety goggles made of plastic,
holding nothing but my breath,
as fumes swirled in the belly
of the flask, digestive juices
consuming their own stomach.

Can a sentence, having moved
from left to right, move
right to left again, taking back
its meaning without trace?
If so, the constant tug of form
and content comes to this:
style turning on substance,
my cut glass snake swallowing
its tail, utterly self-absorbed,
erasing all it ever was.

ROBERT GRAY

I believe poems ought to be able to stand by themselves, without the help of their author's comments. Anyway, artists' statements on their work are almost always overstatements, don't you think? Whatever I point out will become the clichéd approach; whatever I overlook, on this occasion, won't here- after be allowed to be there. Best to leave it to the critics: they're easier to discount. The freshness of a poem is all that is unspoken in it.

The Meatworks

Most of them worked around the slaughtering
out the back, where concrete gutters
crawled off
heavily, and the hot, fertilizer-thick
sticky stench of blood
sent flies mad,
but I settled for one of the lowest-paid jobs, making mince
right the furthest end from those bellowing,
sloppy yards. Outside, the pigs' fear
made them mount one another
at the last minute. I stood all day
by a shaking metal box
that had a chute in, and a spout,
snatching steaks from a bin they kept refilling
pushing them through
arm-thick corkscrews, grinding around inside it,
    meat or not —
chomping, bloody mouth —
using a greasy stick
shaped into a penis.
When I grabbed it the first time
it slipped, slippery as soap, out of my hand,
in the machine
that gnawed it hysterically a few moments
louder and louder, then, shuddering, stopped;
fused every light in the shop.
Too soon to sack me —
it was the first thing I'd done.
For a while, I had to lug gutted pigs
white as swedes
and with straight stick tails
to the ice rooms, hang them by the hooves
on hooks — their dripping
solidified like candle-wax — or pack a long intestine
with sausage meat.
We got meat to take home —
bags of blood;
red plastic with the fat showing through.

We'd wash, then
out on the blue metal
towards town; but after sticking your hands all day
in snail-sheened flesh,
you found, around the nails, there was still blood.
I usually didn't take the meat.
I'd walk home on
the shiny, white-bruising beach, in mauve light,
past the town.
The beach, and those startling, storm-cloud mountains, high
beyond the furthest fibro houses, I'd come
to be with. (The only work
was at this Works.) — My wife
carried her sandals, in the sand and beach grass,
to meet me. I'd scoop up shell-grit
and scrub my hands,
treading about
through the icy ledges of the surf
as she came along. We said that working with meat was like
burning-off the live bush
and fertilizing with rottenness,
for this frail green money.
There was a flaw to the analogy
you felt, but one
I didn't look at, then —
the way those pigs stuck there, clinging onto each other.

A Sight of Proteus

for Ted and Kathy Hillyer

These squat or long-drawn shapes, like toadstool caps,
are sandstone rocks
in silhouette, against a silvery band of ocean
of an afternoon,

as I climb down from the track along the cliff-tops
and pause, on opportunistic steps,
above gravel
in the shingle pits,

that lie below those ramparts on the wide rock tables;
where you can walk
at eye-level
with the running-in of the surf. I look back

along the cliff-face, its facets
grey and fissured
as a Picasso, cubist period,
and see how the bushfire-swift, white surfline ignites

and drives smoke
toward shore, while the sea out from here is a deep navy,
past where the sun props
one arm behind it, and is calm and empty.

Below, the waves dragging off the black rock platform
are a stark root-system,
or a backward-sucked lightning screen,
pronged, a few moments, in relative slow-motion.

Awaiting me, obliquely, is a deserted beach, and those wisps
of she-oak, that complain
delicately, it seems, behind it; and on the low dunes
are beach vines

and the aqua-coloured grass, that leans
onto any breeze,
as compliant as shadows.
The light in the wet shore has a metallic sheen

as if great ventilator shafts
are sunken there. And one can see — braced on the rocks of this corner,
in hope of dolphins —
how the river flatly drifts

parallel with the dunes, and has sand
banked shining within it, and how the mangrove island
is all white birds,
settled there like the chips of light on part of the water.

This river as slowly as possible comes around
to its estuary. The town,
under the headlands' smooth grass haunch and the reservoir,
is the poles for light and telephone,

a block of wooden flats (which I know says Vacancy),
the steep roofs of pub and general store,
a cross, the signs on the hamburger and video joints, and the fibro
or timber houses, climbing from their hollow

with the climbing bitumen,
onto a cleared and scrubby hillside.
The mountains, far beyond, are drawn to left and right,
and their flat facade

is transient
as convolvulus, in colour,
and this affects their form, and their locality,
or it does seemingly.

Earlier, when setting out,
I saw a girl from town run down the shore,
passing her clothes to a friend, and, coiling up her black hair
one-handed, at the last moment,

dive beneath a wave. She swam
easily to where some boardriders had settled in the sun,
then lay back among them,
talking, tilted in the sea that passed,

her body white through the clear surface of those rollers,
the bikini-bottom like a shadow;
and only now
she returns, with the other kids, striding back strongly onto shore.

Sometimes the fishermen work from down there,
using a great net
immemorial style: wading out, while two undo it from a rowing boat
that is the last of its floats,

and they take the catch right at their front door.
They draw
a broad welcoming one-armed embrace upon the water
that turns crushing.

I saw them do this toward evening, as the few boardriders came home,
who rode above the net-hem,
hot-dogging and stylish; and the men, hanging on,
shouted at them,

calling someone a young bastard;
one probably his father.
Some women, sometimes, and other men
from the pub, each of those holding a glass or a beer can,

come and sit in the dunes,
but not much chiacking goes one, as the surf totters
the older workers, thigh-deep, who take the strain, and cuffs the others
in their faces.

They know when a school of fish is about to pass this town
by a fire a lookout will set
a match to, on top of the headland
beneath which I stand. That sight

brings them running from the pub,
while others drive, and hauling their net from a trailer,
carrying it in file —
it is dark as the seaweed along the shore, in its roll.

And when they pick
the fish they want, there on the beach, they pack
these in plastic
and ice, and onto the four-wheel drives, backed up;

which, to an aesthete watching,
is a pity, particularly
the carving-up of the shore; and then they race back
to a cold-room shed, near the railway.

With twilight, the long prow of tumbled-down rock
before this headland
is surrounded by an almost luminescent
foam, constantly elastic;

and a loose breast-pocket handkerchief of whiteness
appears, against black stone,
from time to time, with a notable flourish, and is being re-tucked
as you look again.

Out to sea, the water's become
a rich greenish-grey, oil-streaked it would seem
with violet, and the sky
a dark violet-grey.

And there is something extraordinary sailing by —
an arctic cloud,
shelved and squared, and upreared out of the horizon,
lit from far inland, where the sun has almost disappeared;

blue, apricot and rose veils shifting within its white.
Though, such a sight
fades very soon: the power turned off, it loses splendour and form
as you watch.

And now the low black mountain rim
is gilt-fringed
far along, with the light that has been hived here, progressively,
in the surf, and sealed away.

There's a last surfrider, just there,
and another one, moving from beyond some rocks;
each in the mild air still waiting astride
his board,

although it's invisible, from where I look down.
They seem, in drifting clear
of the shadows, to be giants, who are standing out
amid the sea's tremor, those myriad oil-cups of low blue light.

The closest one, an old hippie, is bald, with a flag-like beard
and a carved build, and he folds his arm
like a Greek sea-god,
who looks in across that blowing hem

to the flimsy town. No longer hidden,
he is considering going ashore, or he longs to, and living in this place
so 'backward' and 'slow',
where the smoky streetlights have come on.

J S HARRY

I'm currently extending the Peter Henry Lepus sequence (from *The Life on Water and the Life Beneath*) in various directions, while continuing to write poetry that is not directly tied to that sequence.

Time In A Pelican's Wing

lake george's
pelicans

stationary
as elders or royal relations

immobilized
by an absence of light

stand formal

like knives & forks
stuck upright
in mud for the night

day will have them up
using themselves
differently

spooning mud
water vegetables
& fish

so what

if they've been having
the flavours of the
lakes they fished in changed

as the nameless
brands of water

were formed & disappeared

on this continent

for 30 or 40 million years

they have followed water
scooping fish frogs crabs to live
to here —

today lake george
        is the clearest of soups —

unknowing

as the tide's pollutants move
        on the shore-crabs
as the effluent flows
        down the rivers & creeks
as the agricultural chemicals
        wash   off the land
into streams

what time is left
        in the flight of their wings —

unlike humans or sun
        they are not
big drinkers of lakes

they will dribble back the water
        keep the fish

we are joined to them by ignorance
what time is left in anyone's drink

Mrs Mothers' Day

i am mrs mothers' day
i will hire myself out to you
for the 364 other days
i will not be satisfied by
1 plus 364
grottybunches of whitechrysanthemum

you choose to offer me snottynose
i will not be placated by
a dinner a picnic
a free ride to the cemetery under yr
dog's blanket to look at a chunk of
white stone & think of yr father
yr father was not
cut stone with a jamjar
stuffed with dying flowers he pissed
on alive flowers more than once said
it was good for them

i will be yr mother
yr motherinlaw
pregnant   lover aunt sister & stranger
doing the splits like a millipede
each foot in a different cliché
yr fantasy of me wife immortally
impregnated by you: sons for ever!
i will even be yr fantasy of
how it feels
to be me sucked by you one minute
you're at my tit then it's yr child's turn
old i mix yr faces up

i will wear my sex like
a great figure with no clothes on it
i will wear my sex like a massive ladywrestler's
figure that you would like to imagine covered
i will wear you like a
loved codpiece with added
imaginative advantages
i will be yr nosewiper yr shelter yr stomach
flatterer racing tipster & bible
on all of the 364 other days
you will not believe my racing tips
till the horses win
i will defend you
against fear of yr impotence
that my competence fosters

for it will neuter us i will be strong
in the war you are in
against yr own obsolescence
for it is my war too

i will cherish you like a glass
of milk soothes yr gut & a greasy hamburger
hits yr ulcer

i will take equal money for my work to the money
you get
give or take a few allowances for sex's
unique variations
i cannot feasibly hire myself out
as a sperm donor

         i will be yr psyche's strength
in the war of yr nerve against the steel man

you are seeing yourself as less than
& unman you by over-fuck after if i am lucky
collecting some child that is wanted

i will pay for you to have sewing lessons to fix
up the holes in yr sox
pump up yr ego & save

every damaged dog cat chicken lizard tadpole
spider duckling you ever
give me to save from its death for yr temporary interest
that i will have to feed & look after for ever

as yr kodak i will not let a thing you think
shames you but i am proud of
slap to the back of the memory-bureau & lie
with its face down matting with the dust of Forgotten
i will preserve the piece of toffee
you made for me in 4th. grade inside the
indian headdress you rejected when you were 10
— which headdress you now
wish to give to yr own son minus toffee —

i will listen to you till yr
voice runs out like bathwater

as yr wife i will never let anyone come between
you & yr mother who is not me

aren't you too stuck on the outskirts
of the day you have set me in
like a cement foot-print outside the theatre?

can we pay
            for us to come inside
                                & play like it is
                        for the rest of the year?
do you really want   to stick neon lights in my cunt
& worship there   for the 364   other days?

now it's
            yr turn   (off stage)   sotto nervous
who   do you want   me to be   what do you *think* to say
now that i've gone?

An Impression of Minimalist Art in the Late Twentieth Century

A yellow
semi-deflated balloon
floats trapped
on a small
green circle
of water surrounded
by white
water lilies. Jagged
reeds fence the outer
water circle of it,
making palisade. Wind
would stretch
this balloon's rubber luck
thin as a condom
around nothing, pressing it up

against the submerged
pricks of the
flattened
fallen palm fronds.
It breaks with a soft
plosive,
sigh or an exhalation,
leaving no children.

The burst balloon's rubber
drifts slowly
down centuries of water
past the forms
of the swirling eels
and the sucking mouths
of their skinny offspring.
Going down without a self
through the centuries
it is seen as a yellow flower
or a floating petal
on a water lily garden
at Giverny. In the late
twentieth century,
it's ok, don't cry;
it is rubber!
Perfectly hygienic
to wear against the skin
to suck
or to throw away.
Ego leaves a mark on it
redundant as the whorls
of the first,
artist's finger prints.

KEVIN HART

Poetry is an experience of limits: it travels around the border-lines of what can be named and what must be left unnamed. It does not betray these borders: it respects their mystery and complexity. The best conductor of mystery is clarity. The true bearer of complexity is simplicity.

Gypsophila

Another day with nothing to say for itself —
Gypsophila on the table, a child's breath
When breath is all it has to name the world

And therefore has no world. It must be made:
Her shadow sleeping on the wall, the rain
That pins fat clouds to earth all afternoon,

A river playing down the piano's scales.
This is the strangest of all possible worlds
With foam upon the beach, the sea's dead skin,

And lightning quietly resting in each eye.
Like gypsy camps or love, it must be made,
Undone, then made again, like the chill rain

That falls without hope of climbing back,
Content to leave its mark, for what it is,
Upon the window or in the child's mind.

Gypsophila on the table, rain outside,
The child will tune the world to her desire
And make another world to keep in mind:

These breaths of air in which we softly wrap
The rain's glass stems to let them fall again
In sunlight, or flower for ever in the mind.

A world of things with nothing at all to say,
A margin that absorbs our silences:
The child must take the lightning from her eye

And place it in the sky, her shadow must
Be told to fall asleep. This strangest world
In which we say *Gypsophila, Baby's breath* —

Three Prayers

Master of energy and silence
    Embracer of contradictions
Who withdraws behind death
    Like horizons we never touch
Who can be One and Many
    Like light refracting through glass,

Stepping in and out of logic
    Like a child unsure of the sea
In and out of time
    Like an old man dozing, waking,
In and out of history
    Like a needle through cloth,

Who we chase and bother with theories
    Who hides in equations and wind
Who is constant as the speed of light
    Who stretches over the Empty Place
Who hangs the Earth upon Nothing
    Who strikes like lightning.

~

Master of Light, my God,
Before whom stars tremble
And fall into themselves,

Who glows within each thing
Beyond reach of language
And deeper than silence,

Who passes through the Dark
That draws us towards death
And makes it one with you,

Whose Light is everywhere
Wherein I stand and see
My shadow disappear.

~

You do not speak to me of death,
You do not pester me, like some.

Far too busy with the universe,
Sometimes not busy enough,

Searching out our softer parts,
Trying to squeeze yourself in:

Showing off your famous night sky
Like a child with a new drawing,

Forever posing impossible problems
We try to solve like crosswords:

So when I wake and see the ceiling
Mottled like an old man's skin

I think of you,
When I imagine the grinning dead

I think of you,
And also when, at night,

I sometimes wake to find
A hand slowly stroking my thigh.

Membranes

1

A voice, almost a voice, in the wee hours
When no one else is home: a body turns
And feels its comprehension of the bed,
An ear affirms the silence of its house

And only then admits a pounding heart.
Heat sits in judgement over everyone,
O Lord, this summer night whose rising up
And going down give cruel sleep at best:

Each louvre set to catch the storm's cracked air
And old verandahs slung out round the back
All drenched with moonlight and mosquito nets.
Tough kids are fucking in the high school yard

While traffic whispers on the Ipswich Road;
A train bears empty carriages out west,
The river sighs while passing Mandalay.
There was no voice. That girl from years ago

Was not about to speak before you woke.
Ah, let her go. And let those other souls
With cold, fixed eyes of dolls left under beds
Go home, o let them slip into the dark …

A voice, almost a voice, though not a voice:
Something between the mind and night, perhaps,
Something that tries to speak but always fails
And leaves a memory with nothing there.

2

To walk all day beside the lazy river,
Beginning from its loop at Blackheath Road
And vaguely heading down to Cockatoo,
A full canteen of ice slung round my neck,

Then cutting back at four down bolted paths
That open, suddenly, onto thick bush
Or spiky fences running fast for miles
At Wacol Prison or the 'Private Road':

It was somewhere round there I lost my way,
Some Sunday when the mercury went mad,
And found a factory defunct for years
With grass that grew right through the broken glass,

And I remember climbing up and down
And gulping thick warm water with a taste
Of tin and leather from my father's war,
And I recall a sign that said 'Condemned'

Through cobwebs, swastikas and clumsy hearts,
And red brick dust that ran beneath my nails
And loud mosquitoes ripping up my arms,
The walls all going wavy in the heat,

And none of it adds up to anything,
Only a nameless fear that sometimes leaps
From nowhere on these summer evenings:
Just coming to; no stars; a drip of blood;

The sweat already cold upon my back,
And drunken voices flapping in the wind,
And someone, me, now smashing through the bush
And leaving someone, me, still sleeping there.

3

Half-dreaming of desire, or solitude,
I thought, Apollo Bay: arriving there
One winter evening while driving west
And drinking dirty water from a hose

Then clambering around the breakwater
With a kind girl I didn't love enough:
The fishing ships at ease, a massive hill
Intent on brooding over all the bay

And moving closer, so it seemed, as night
Came home at last, but slowly, wave on wave.
Nowhere more beautiful than here, I thought,
(A sorrow old as all the stars was out

And roaming round the bay, as though it knew
Our bodies were both made of stars). No time
More radiant than now: her fingertips
Just touching near her mouth, and ocean waves

Returning once again in their good time
While I was nearly breathing her warm breath.
A moment that unfolds and makes a life,
A moment surely reaching out to — no,

Not that, I thought, not that, and then stepped back.
An icy breeze was on the loose, and so
'As Goethe said', I said, and she agreed,
And there was somewhere else we had to go.

4

i.m. G.H.

The train is skimming Maryland at night
When you are called back home. But who? And where?
You look outside, and someone there looks back.
It's you, thank God, well almost — yes, it is,

And sleep belongs to someone else's life
And that was you as well, or nearly. No:
Old questions breathe beside you as you wake
And bring old answers slowly to their knees.

Snow falls on roads where you will never walk,
On trees that you will never sit beneath;
It was her face you saw out in the night
And she was whispering a word. Lost, lost,

Forever lost, and waves pass over you:
A mountain, and a wine glass being filled,
A long embrace and then a sudden look
That cancels years and years. Well it was her.

And so her dying enters into you;
After a year or more of clenching hard
At last it happens, all that void at once,
Its full enormous rush against the heart

With people all around awake, asleep,
Some counting minutes till they open doors
And others reading Bibles with a pen,
And no one here can take the truth away,

Not the conductor in his uniform,
Not the dark face that looks at you outside.
O let her go the train wheels start to chant
But to the dark you whisper *No no no* —

DENNIS HASKELL

A whole aesthetic — although not a very exact one — is contained in a statement which Ezra Pound pinched from the Chinese, and which is the most important thing ever said about poetry: 'Only emotion endures'. We live in a poetic age infatuated with intellectual cleverness, with experiment for its own sake and with modish, surface effects. It is perhaps because I work in a university that I hate all these attitudes. I seek to write a poetry that incorporates ideas but never ostentatiously, that values ordinary elements in 'ordinary' lives, and that presents all this with as quiet as possible verbal skill, and in a way that evokes the deepest emotions. I aim to do this without slickness, easy irony or surface effects, and without entering the perpetual child's garden of gimmickry known as the 'avant garde'. Above all, I don't want to write Literature.

Poetry is crucial because even in a visual culture besotted with spectacle the great majority of our understanding of the world and of ourselves comes through language, and because poetry is language under the greatest pressure. Poetry thus provides the fullest possible expression of our beings, capable sometimes of expressing meaning apparently beyond the capacity of language. All this sounds incurably Romantic, but I actually believe it. Perhaps I can condition this Romanticism by saying that I want a poetry which seems part of ordinary life, and that, as Philip Larkin said, 'at bottom poetry, like all art, is inextricably bound up with giving pleasure'.

On Sitting Down to deconstruct John Forbes once again

Truculent urbanity leaves the rapid field
and short fuses of sure-fire sense
apparently to enlarge our perceptions, as a bird in the bush
is worth ten in the hand.
But start where you like; I'm on holidays and
it's like wandering around in a lively daze
or flinging a boomerang into the mulga:
it never comes back,
no matter how your intellect crackles
or how surfing championships are won
by effervescent, sun-bronzed Aussies,
with boards lost in Peru.
Boomerang contests are won by Yanks:
it's official, it's on t.v.

You'll never be hooked by a cultural context
no matter what your visa says, or
how long you're staying. You won't be here! or there!
— no matter where you are.
What wond'rous life in this I lead;
Bright similes drop about my head!
All your veins like a show in Vegas,
the panache is undeniable. Hooked on nerves,
opening the book's like opening a Pepsi
or plugging a fuse into the box
with the power on: it always fizzes, no matter what the
expiry date, it froths like a machine.

Cape Fear

Sex, the black pit of ourselves,
drags me by the hand
and we stump along the coast
where an ocean of delight keeps up
against the sucking jaws of sand.
In a sky of ridiculously brilliant light
a small plane flies like a metal gull;
its one, black, angular
footprint running over hills of sand
impotent impressions.

As we walk
the miles-thick ocean builds up
its battery of emptiness, and arches
watery, knuckleduster fists
which beat the flanks
of desire white and blue.
We walk through its frothing aftermath
where hard-packed sand
breaks each fist
into untiring fingers
that feel their way up the curves of shore
and cannot grip, and slip back
and back and back, and arch again,
the endless thrush and bash of ocean
running up our legs
a ceaseless, bruising foam.

And I recall the rock-filled road
I have just travelled,
strewn with kangaroo carcasses
and green splattered parrots.
In my shade-netted square of garden
black-pipe-guided water drips
and insects swarm to my legs.
Thick and dark as hair they feed.

How the world sees us is how
we see the world,
its violence so brilliant
that all we can do is enter and belong.
These are the rigours of the age,
the consequence of life lived in the head,
its love of fear, its violet distance from sense,
its fascinating reward, its post-modern brilliance.

Evening Flight

We left the hazy city
in fretting light
and lost each house,
each line of fence,
each shine of office,
the fluctuating fingerprints
of wind on water
beneath their harvest of rain

and soared into a tiffin
surrealism, above the clouds,
sunset shining over
great crevasses of sky
where distance moved faster
than hours, slurped up
by the mysterious techniques of engines,
their arithmetic of air,

which encouraged in us a shared, introverted,
listless riding and biding of time.
Here to touch each other
might be to handle the flesh of clouds.

Only the now and then shuddering
suggested a world outside

where the body aches
and only occasionally smiles.
The prickly blue carpet
is lined with stars,
night or day,
and I wondered
what could give meaning
to the insistent
inadequacies of flesh,
to our pampered, pudgy,
diminutive lives

now shining inside
while the wing tilts
a blank slab of dark
end-tipped with fragile light.
In commitment to comfort, and suspended,
everybody's mind is lined with death.

Romanticism in the 1990s

Yachts
like gulls with upturned wings
alone in their element
silently flit across
a fine horizon
of thin, listless cloud.
On the shore we stare out to sea
amongst the translucent
blobs of jellyfish foam,
sand sinking into our toes.
And the yachts look like elegance,
delicacy of action.

Wind spits along the groyne
as they startle west
away from us
across the brackish chop,
chimeras billowing colour
before a salt-laden blast.

But here they are
suddenly wrenched towards us
direct, heaving slowly,
relentlessly onward.
Spinnakers grow flaccid
and are roped in.
Bony hulls lift
less and less often
from the water.
The wind comes in clots.
The closer and closer
they get to us
the more they become
big, lumbering boats.

Unsuccessful Interview

I'm blessed to discover my smallness.
            — Thea Astley, *Reaching Tin River*

To be brought in under the guise of praise
has your self flower like lushest jungle,

grass and trees a rich deep green, the lilies
of intrinsic admiration floating on the pond

of the tranquil ego.
You soar into this enquiry into you,

hope in your luggage, significance present
but strangely on hold:

after all, this is Australia.
Going back it should be no surprise

to find, above the runnelled, red-baked land
as hard as fate, the lumpy cracks

surrounded by dust, the sun-shattered rock,
that you are as empty as air,

and winds blowing through the thin-fleeced cloud
need no further strength to miff

the puff of self, to sing on and on
in the endless and possibly meaningless blue.

DOROTHY HEWETT

A modernist interested in symbolism, imagism and surrealism, I published my first poems in 1941 when I was only eighteen. They didn't seem to bear any resemblance to other Australian poetry, but I was reading D H Lawrence, Pound, Eliot, Edith Sitwell, Dylan Thomas and Hart Crane.

In the late fifties, trying for communication, I wrote several literary ballads and long narrative poems influenced by Whitman's striding muscular line.

In the seventies and eighties, under the influence of Lowell's *Life Studies* and Berryman's *Dream Songs*, I moved into a period of personal lyrics and family sagas, writing poems about sexual love and political disillusionment. Later with Creeley's minimalist poems and O'Hara's seemingly throwaway lines, I experimented with the brief, short, jagged moment.

I have never been particularly interested in distance or objectivity, but amongst my poems in those years were several reworked myths and fairytales to illustrate female sexuality.

These days I am revisiting, and trying to illuminate, small moments of domestic experience, working on them until each moment carries an extra freight of meaning, but has a note as crystal as a tuning fork. I think that these new, brief, deceptively simple poems, made from remembered moments of childhood experience, are probably the fruits of old age when childhood comes back in a blaze of recognition. Like my dreams they are full of ghosts, and will be published in a new book entitled *Half-way up the Mountain*.

I am rather suspicious of statements about my own poetry. Like Gig Ryan I think a poem should stand on its own feet.

Psyche's Husband

He is the Monster-husband who comes
to Psyche in the darkness of her wish-palace.
    — Robert Duncan, *The Truth and Life of Myth*

In the darkness of the myth-palace I sit waiting
the feast is laid the tapers lit   the musak plays
the crow sharpens & taps a beak on the iron cradle
along the marble halls I can hear paws dragging
a giant shadow falls
the baby cries with the wind in its christening robes
& the beast is upon me
the stink from its snout   its sad pig eyes
its fur ripples along my skin
kiss me   it sobs   melodious-voiced   *kiss me*

I run shrieking through the palace
as I snatch up the child the crow pecks at my wrists
the carpet lifts with the draughts under the doors
the air-conditioner   humming   is set up high
I look back only once
there is a toad with a horned head
sadly plopping down the stairs behind me
kiss me   it croaks   *kiss me*
the crow drinks my blood on the doormat
that spells   WELCOME

now I live in the woodcutter's cottage
nodding in the peaceful kingdom
sometimes I hear the crow squawking
as it scans the canopy of leaves above my head
the toad squats & snaps in the marshes
the glamorous roar of the beast hums under my feet

my son with the beast's snout   the toad's horn
& the crow's claw snuffles for acorns
along the floor of the rainforest
kiss me   he snorts   *kiss me.*

The Murderers

When we were children
we were in love with death
we buried our dolls in the winter
and dug them up in the spring
they were the brides of Hades
the daughters of Dis
their washed-out eyes
had seen strange things
                    in the earth.

Sometimes we dug and dug
and couldn't find them
like the murderer
in the Belanglo Forest
we forgot where we put them
the backpacking dolls
smiling from photographs
their taped mouths screaming
their hands tied up with wire
the cracked china dolls
their glass eyes rattling
the dancing dolls beheaded
clutching each other
under last year's leaves ...

scratching arrows in bark
stumbling from tree to tree
whispering their names
we searched from season to season
for our lost dolls.

The Brothers

Those ghostly brothers that I never had
larger than life stalking the countryside
their spittle darkening the dust
ungainly men who never married
clodhopping through barbed fences
looping furrows   their shorn ewes
bleating in a ring of crows
the film of ice cracks on the handbasin
the dough rises in a drone of flies.
I meet them in the paddocks in the evening
standing like fence posts in a line of sorrow
they never speak but weather in the glow
a band of light edging the earth's curve.

Living Dangerously

O to live dangerously again,
meeting clandestinely in Moore Park,
the underground funds tucked up between our bras,
the baby's pram stuffed with illegal lit.
We hung head down for slogans on the Bridge,
the flatbed in the shed ran ink at midnight.

Parked in the driveway, elaborately smoking,
the telltale cars, the cameras, shorthand writers.
Plans for taking over ... 3 yrs the revolution.
The counter revs. out gunning for the cadres.
escape along the sea shelf, wading through
                warm waters soft with Blood.
wow! what a story! ... guerilla fighters
wear cardigans and watch it on The Box,
lapsed Party cards, and Labor's in again.

Retired, Comrade X fishes Nambucca Heads,
& Mrs Petrov, shorthand typist,
              hiding from reporters
            brings home the weekly bacon.

But   O   O   O to live
             so dangerously again,
their Stamina trousers pulling at the crutch.

Lady's Choice

So there he is in the mirror again
his armour glistening with tears or rain
and I am expected to leave the room
to take three paces and then go down
to the water's edge where the lilies blow
the boat's turned turtle the bright tides
                  flowing
fast and free but I'm not going
to give myself to that waiting crowd
staring and nudging their thoughts aloud
while he stands there pontificating
on God and mercy and grace and faces
better to turn my back and stare
over the meadows of luminous air
thinking tomorrow I'll get up early
work on my poems and thread my loom
won't speak to strangers be brief and surly
cover the mirror and choose my end
not death in the town round the river's bend
but here cold-hearted alone in my room.

Once I Rode with Clancy ...

Once I rode with Clancy through the wet hills of Wickepin,
By Kunjin and Corrigin with moonlight on the roofs,
And the iron shone faint and ghostly on the lonely moonlit siding
And the salt earth rang like crystal underneath our flying hoofs.

O once I rode with Clancy when my white flesh was tender,
And my hair a golden cloud along the wind,
Among the hills of Wickepin, the dry salt plains of Corrigin,
Where all my Quaker forebears strove and sinned.

Their black hats went bobbing through the Kunjin churchyard,
With great rapacious noses, sombre-eyed,
Ringbarked gums and planted pine trees, built a raw church
In a clearing, made it consecrated ground because they died.

From this seed I spring — the dour and sardonic Quaker men,
The women with hooked noses, baking bread,
Breeding, hymning, sowing, fencing off the stony earth,
That salts their bones for thanksgiving when they're dead.

It's a country full of old men, with thumbscrews on their hunger,
Their crosses leaning sideways in the scrub.
My cousins spit to windward, great noses blue with moonlight,
Their shoulders propping up the Kunjin pub.

O once I rode with Clancy through the wet hills of Wickepin,
By Kunjin and Corrigin with moonlight on the roofs,
And the iron shone faint and ghostly on the lonely, moonlit siding
And the salt earth rang like crystal underneath our flying hoofs.

And the old men rose muttering and cursed us from the graveyard
When they saw our wild white hoofs go flashing by,
For I ride with landless Clancy and their prayers are at my back,
They can shout out strings of curses on the sky.

By Wickepin, by Corrigin, by Kunjin's flinty hills,
On wild white hoofs that kindle into flame,
The river is my mirror, the wattle tree our roof,
Adrift across our bed like golden rain.

Let the old men clack and mutter, let their dead eyes run with rain,
I hear the crack of doom across the scrub,
For though I ride with Clancy there is much of me remains,
In that moonlit dust outside the Kunjin pub.

My golden hair has faded, my tender flesh is dark,
My voice has learned a wet and windy sigh
And I lean above the creek bed, catch my breath upon a ghost,
With a great rapacious nose and sombre eye.

CORAL HULL

I want to tell it like it is, then have something done about it.

Sharpies

we decide to have a picnic/ on the way home from
school/ we settle down/ beneath a council gum/ in
front of someone's frontyard/ diane spreads out a
brown & yellow checkered tea towel/ over december
thistles & hidden bindis/ it is very hot/ the tea
towel is soft against our legs/ our uniforms short/
we have saved half our lunch/ diane's homemade cup
cakes/ with sour mock cream/ half a plastic bottle
of iced red cordial/ a vegemite sandwich on thick
white bread/ two chocolate wheatens wrapped in wax
paper & a soapy orange/ diane has saved her salt 'n'
vinegar chip crumbs/ i liked them the best/ because
that's where the flavour was strongest/ i always
said: save me the crumbs diane/ save me the crumbs/
& she always did/ we picked a quiet street/ off gill
avenue/ in case our parents came looking for us/
more than likely/ it would be diane's parents/ who
were over protective/ & we ate/ & we gossiped/ &
no one bothered us/ & then it was 5.30 p.m./ we packed
up real quick/ & diane went home & got into trouble/
& when i got home/ mum was cleaning the kitchen
blinds/ & she didn't even look at me/ as she asked:
where have you been?/
                              our primary school relief
teacher/ mrs hay/ tells us/ that she keeps a lot of
cats/ she is fifty years old/ she sits in front of
the class/ her legs wide apart/ & tells us stories/
& we could all see her undies/ big white ones/ with
thick elastic/ & there was blood/ on the front of
them/ none of us knew what had happened to her/ she
was so big & old/ & so boisterous/ none of us talked
whilst she was talking/ mrs hay tells us/ about
girls 'n' boys being kidnapped/ & put into glad bags/
into car boots/ & about their underpants/ & what
had been done to them/ & about the mother crying
on the news who said/ that her little girl/ always had
a clean frock on/ & her father who said: i washed her
socks every night/ children dumped/ in ditches/ off
the road/ down by shady creeks/ where no one went/

in their singlets/ & underpants/ mrs hay says: never
talk to strangers/ & warren lewington asks: is the
easter bunny okay?/ & was santa okay/ to talk to at
christmas?/ & she never answered straight off/ &
suddenly/ none of us really knew how safe the easter
bunny was/
       friday afternoon/ after school/ diane's
mother gets tiddly/ & cooks us raspberry jam tarts/
she tells us about strangers/ & what they do to
children/ on school holidays/ my grandmother/ makes
me pray for lost children/ last seen together/ a
brother & sister & friend/ on a beach/ in south
australia/ their parents looking for them/ & me
praying/ that jesus/ friend of all children/ would
bring them back/ diane's mother tells us/ how they
find the skulls of children/ buried in the bush/ &
sometimes little pairs of grey school shorts/ &
another time a boy's tooth/ he must have been very
frightened/ he must have run through the bush/ to
get away/ children run a lot/ & mostly are very fast/
at school/ we practise our running in the playground/
& we climb the monkey bars/ we pretend that a
sharpie is after us/ & some of the older kids/ show
me a sharpie's footprint/ embedded in the stone roof/
of the girls' toilets/ i could just about make it out/
but then a big huntsman/ scampered out of a corner/
& we all screamed & ran out into the playground to
play hopscotch/
       at playlunch/ we stand along the
wire fence/ on the very edge/ of the school
playground/ on sharpie patrol/ the teachers had
told us/ to keep an eye out for sharpies/ & to
report any sightings/ to the local head mistress/
no one could be trusted/ gnarled old women/ with
their shopping trolleys/ waved at us/ from across
the street/ passing truck drivers/ honked their
horns/ on their way through/ to the blue mountains/
& we all jumped up & down & squealed in the wind/
then we got bored with looking for sharpies & played
skipping/ at home time/ the german busdriver/ who
makes us sit three to a seat/ who sometimes squashes
us four to a seat/ even though half the bus is empty/

so that the corners of our square brown school bags/
scratch our legs/ well/ we call him 'sharpie'/ because
that is exactly what a sharpie would do/ if he was
a busdriver/ & when he is not working/ for neville's
private bus company/ we know he is a sharpie

Praying Mantis

my father's back to me/ digging in the front garden/
with a spade/ planting the jagged concrete pieces
in/ & introduced trees later to be trimmed/ & fat
cold earthworms to be split by the hook/ i watched
as he unearthed a giant praying mantis/
                                        as green
as the front lawn ripe with insect movement & heat/
like the sound of concrete & grass whistling if the
hose was left running on it/ the mantis faced my
father standing upright & began to box the shadow
of a huge man/
              dad stopped digging with a breath
out & raised his left hand/ the mantis swayed from
side to side as if trying to confuse my father or
duck blows/ suddenly i saw the mantis as six feet
high & my father as quite small/
                                 i grabbed hold of
guenther's hand & took him around the side trellis/
i told him the new word/ i whispered: my father is
a shit/ guenther's thin blonde hair pricked his ear
as he jumped/ like when i asked my nan about the
word cunt/ who told you that word?/ the kids at
school/ well it's a very bad word/
                                  i looked up at
her/ is it worse than fuck?/ yes it's a very very
bad word/ so don't let me catch you saying it/ &
stop picking your nose or it will end up like a
black fella's/ & don't go cross eyed or the wind
will change direction/

& be good or santa won't
come/ & don't cry or the disprin won't work/ & don't
be naughty or god will punish you/ guenther went &
told my father/ who looked about to sweep the mantis
into oblivion with the spade/ instead dad threw it
down on the grass clippings/
       & i raced inside to my
bedroom/ & hid behind the wooden door & his heavy
footsteps down the hallway/ he knocked me down with
blows to the head/ black thuds to a red face on a
short green dress/
       outside i could imagine guenther
satisfied/ & i knew the praying mantis would be
swaying to the breeze/ about to take flight/ a
moment away from death/ on razor edged legs/
barely touching down on the upturned earth

21. The Secret Horses of Peterborough, South Australia

they are receiving hate mail at the peterborough knackery,
25,000 feet above sea level, for the destruction at the heart of an australian
   legend,
it takes a certain type of human being to kill a horse for profit,
then to become addicted to it and to kill a hundred million horses in a lifetime,
a lifetime's worth of horse killing decided upon,

some were solitary, limping on the hard compacted dirt, trodden down,
others had formed herd hierarchies and short term friendships,
they all starved and were thirsty in the outdoor waiting room,
the head manager said, 'what we do with the horses is ours and ours only,'
there were five diseased camels, slack in the neck, too defeated to graze,
the guy at the post office said, 'camels were on last week,'
now the horses and camels looking at me from the colour slides are all dead,

the plant manager wouldn't tell me anything, no photos inside or outside,
then no answering questions,
but we all know what they are doing, the bastards, hush, sshhh, silence,

it's a very sensitive industry,
we have to watch our backs, and so they should, horse-killers,
there's a definite S.A. feeling to it, suppression of information leaving the
    knackery,
'what's that smoke?' 'you're good aren't you?'
'well it aint firewood you're burnin' in there buddy,'

the racing industry is largely responsible for horses living out the rest of
    their lives
as mince, out the back in the holding yards, barren, straw and dust,
dozens of children's dreams left unattended, crippled legs, shaggy manes,
i want to get all those horses and take them home, as life long
companions, gorgeous browns,

the strict chill in the crunchy sugar of the bones of horses,
a wind that howls down the bare sides of those frosty gullies,
horses stand in the holding yards freezing to death at night,
frozen to the bone, it sinks in, a cold that penetrates and aches,
long grasses are blown towards sunset in-between those hills,
down along the windy road the rabbits follow the heat down,
thornbills hop in the mistletoe as the frost comes up to settle,
this is winter in south australia where the horses are slaughtered,

filmy eyed horses that have seen too much, transportation truck survivors
privately concealed, the secrecy surrounding the operation, the gaunt moon
clandestine horses, confidential, quiet,
these starving limping horses, with sores on their fine strong legs,
it's all hush-hush,

from the distance i saw the hose whip being lifted to move unwilling horses
into the process and horses rearing up, i saw their manes and gorgeous
    heads
up thrown and knew that their hooves would be smashing down,
they did not want to go in,

i look down at my own forearms, my chest cavity, hands, thighs, muscles,
    bones, blood
racing through the organs, in moments i will be chopped down to mince

without a head,
this is all i am, what it has down come to, downed like horses, pulped for
    profit,

the secret horses of peterborough; minutes later
they were viewing the slaughter of the horses in front,
seconds later, choking on their own blood, they die silently, then are thick
    smoke,
they are horses unpublished, encoded, cryptic,

i will find the information on the exhausted outskirts, of horses with no hope,
the humps of camels, in the bare distance, that rose above the barrier,
silhouetted on their way into the process,
nobody wants to get to know a scraggly old camel
and these tired, mangy horses, nobody's pets, no child's dream anymore,

the horse butchers; knew well to guard their secret,
the slaughter of horses slaughters some dream inside all of us,
there is something about a horse-killer,
i live for beauty only to find it being destroyed by the knackery,
everything is falling into it, everything,
the bare hills of peterborough, the heart of the town,

for although it is situated on the outskirts, as most places of massacre are,
the town is dragged into it sideways, sneakily, unwillingly,
the metro meatworks is not out far enough to be hushed up,
the stench of horse flesh wafts in from the sect,
we smell the camels falling, the trees fall into it,
the men's hearts who operate it fall in,
and they are spiritually mangled, by their own machinery,
the world should know about the gulping knackery,

here life is not awarded the simplest curiosity, compassion is obsolete,

the horse-killer bosses with mobile phones are on planes from adelaide
to perth and sydney for board meetings, they are professionals; yet simply
horse-killers and the meetings contain profit from agony,
life means nothing to them, why must it always appear that hate and evil have
the upper hand, that horses will ultimately be disadvantaged,
all i am is flesh and bone, a lover of horses,

the horse-killers can't see beyond their own greed and stupidity,

i want them to go down, to be trampled by hooves of horses going in,
i want the last thing they see, to be those secret hills, their own hostile
    machinery,
i want their flesh as frost, the rabbits and sheep to crush it down,
the sun the next morning to bring it up, until it is made pure, morning good,

i got depressed and trusted no one for a few days after that,
went to bed early to escape the knackery, it was deeply cold,
the wind howled late into the night and into the early hours,
i woke up the next morning and knew of its existence again,

on the way into peterborough, the bare sheep exposed to the elements on
    those hills,
was just a lead into a greater cruelty,
the head manager said, that horses arrived from everywhere at anytime,
he wouldn't tell me things a primary school child would know, hostility and
    suspicion,
he was nervous about the tree types,
about the stench of horse blood running through the office,
faint traces in the tea and biscuit tin,

he said, 'sorry we couldn't help you with more information,
but we received hate mail, when we started doing horses,'
the horses would see the two legged creeps, the knife man coming, the
humming, rock'n'roll
transistor, before the quick slide into blood and terror,
'not killing 'em, no, we do 'em, we do 'em good and proper,'
peterborough is enwrapped in it and this must affect it,
its horses, its children, its town spirit

S K KELEN

I write poems of place and movement — anywhere and every-where from the molecular to the interstellar — which may involve a modicum of pace, but there are also poems of still-ness and meditation. My lifelong aim is to explore and marvel at the world and make poetry from those explorations. My travel poems work by engaging the many societies I have had the good fortune to visit, and go beyond to the land's reso-nances and the myths that arise from the land. They celebrate a world that is still beautiful and exciting — but is under many toxic threats — celebrate its many and diverse cultures and landscapes. Though the poems seek the mystical, they do not retreat from engaging life's darker sides or despatching a tyrant with wit. Whether fast-paced or still, my poems seek a unity of vision. Geopolitics, landscapes of longing, the crea-tures of life and imagination ... discussing one's approach to the art of poetry can sound like voodoo, or worse. I reckon poetry's a warrior thing — what that means is hard to say, it's an intuitive statement. That's why occasionally when wildness calls, it might be wise to answer. Revelation can happen in the backyard or on a mountain top, in dreams or at the office, on the highways or watching children play: where poems are born. The future of poetry? One day when humans make the great trip to the stars, a cosmonaut may feel the need to take a breather with an ancient twentieth or twenty-first century pastoral, urban or rural — for a reminder of the bright beauty of Earth and the greatness of her oceans, deserts, forests and cities, to seek inspirational words in times of trouble or just for fun — and opening a book they will find happiness in the timeless field of poetry. I hope the kids growing up on Mars Colony will get the opportunity to read and enjoy some of my poems.

S K KELEN

The Spin of the Dice

A green Mallarmé floats ethereal over
the Harbour Bridge so I

set out for Canberra, hopeful of
poems — big pink shiny ones.

Goodbye sweetheart, I'm off in my happy
red sports car and crazy blue shoes

driving over murdered blackfellas' bones
thinking of bunkum and myself

amidst the better known Greek gods.
It rains then I turn on the Sony

stereo eight-track cartridge-player
and Dylan's dirge comes out

in the full glory of stereo, though
it would be better if the higher treble

notes were clearer. I should have
bought a car cassette-player instead of

the cartridge player, could have bought
one with a Dolby noise-reduction system

and used the cassettes from
the cassette deck in the hi-fi system.

I stop at Bermagui and trying not to be obscure
eat cabanossi for breakfast remembering Eluard,

Kafka, Joyce, Frank Kermode, the Furies,
and Dylan's words: I ain't gonna work on Maggie's farm

no more.

Mid-West 1

Bathed in unlucky blood
Bison land is stamped by a bitumen
Web enmeshing sacred ground,
State shields glint blue in the sun

So the free spirit changes gear
Fuel-injected, turbo charged,
Chants the sky's tyre mantra:
Wrecked-Auto-Heaven
Smile down on the State & Interstate
Give us frantic, highway joy
At 90 mph you're sure, rip roar the night away.
Carburettors breathe the eagle's country,
There's no speed limit when oneness is reached
And highways meridian industry and peace.
Engines surge, melt mountain
At dawn the trains whistle like ghosts.

Directions

Words flame, rise from the sea &
cities out of the mouths of babes
echo on the mountains
intimated by animals and
the silence of galactic spaces.
Love sighs and laughs
words colour in the background
swirl computers, mass production
ideology, bucolic dreams, machine guns
and TV sets fly into the Sun.
Towns grow dusty as automobiles gleam
with miles and miles of everything.
Life in factories or what Prime Ministers

should say: Angels, dirt, ecstasy,
and poisoned apples.
Asking a girl to a corroboree
is dangerous music that's
o so lovingly subversive
invoking grand schemes.
Quick, let's save the world just for fun!
Dryads dance through the trees.
It is and always will be ...

House of Rats

They're up there, all right,
In the roof playing scrabble, listening to
Scratchy old Fats Waller records.
They started out as a gang of desperadoes
Escaped from a laboratory,
Arrived via a garbage truck
Up overhanging tree branches
Elbowed their way in & soon
The colony is an empire of rats
Who eat the insulation batts
Chew wires, through the ceiling
To ransack the kitchen
Take bites out of everything
& carry off furniture. I can hear them
Scurrying with bits & pieces, hammering & sawing:
They're building houses — a model rat town — with
Imitation garages to park stolen toy cars in.
After munching down another box
Of double strength poison
The rats are back at work with a vengeance, thump
Around the rafters insulating the house with rat shit.
Or hard at love writhing, squealing
Like sick starlings or kicked puppies. The weaker explode
And TV screens fill with rats' blood but there's
More where they came from. Teeming over

Mountains, down valleys, jamming highways, falling
Off bridges to scurry ashore up storm water drains.
Exterminators arrive dressed as astronauts and poison
The house for ten thousand years. It's time to move out.
But the rats have laid eggs in your pockets, stow
Away, follow you from house to house.
The curse enters its exponential phase.
Tentacles unwind from the ceiling, dirty great moths
And leopard slugs take over your happy home.
Soon you are a trellis. That's just what the rats say.
I'm down here listening to radio messages,
Oiling automatic weapons, building rockets.
Living in a rat's belly.

Megalong Valley

The gods banned machines from ever entering
the last pure tract of Megalong.
Here, even bracken's picturesque
& the whipbird, breathless
with the beauty of it all
is silent, reverential.
Splashing a rainbow
there's a waterfall
you walk under
that's always there and will be
until the earth or sun shifts
sandstone cliffs, a kookaburra
laughs from gorgeous gloom
up & down, up & down.

S K KELEN

Tycoon

It's been a great year for news
& buying newspapers
installing a clown
as President
taking over most everything.
And now I own the lot
the experiment can begin
so I'm on my way to pick up
the cloned alien DNA to mix
in with the newsprint
and rubbing readers' fingers
whatever happens will quickly take effect .

Morning birds sing the alarm clock song.
Everything's done: the morning edition
throbs with a signature I'm giving to life.
This holiday's well and truly earned,
the jet's ready, the girls, an island of honey.
On the way to the airport the engine seizes
What does it profit a man jolts heart
and the driver slams brakes.
Something about Gethsemane
and a blinding light, a genie (or is it an angel)
says it's time to earn back soul and life.
Cruel world snuffs out the last candle
— almost — delicious flames lick just enough
now the junket begins in sleaze
where kids on suicide mission
guide a grand tour of body fission.
A poster for a cholera safari catches my eye
at the crook café as I search the classifieds for real estate
to invest in around the burning lake
and order another glass of lava.
The waiters wink, never return with that drink.
I wait and wait until the world dissolves.
God is scattering me sun to sun,
planets pass through my dust belly
and Heaven's gate is ancestors' laughter.
Whistle and speed up the seasons,
come, come o summer.

JOHN KINSELLA

I'm particularly interested in the 'radical pastoral' — in blending the so-called pastoral tradition with the linguistically innovative. This 'hybrid' ironises the pastoral construct but allows for genuine movement through rural spaces. Landscape is central to my project — ways of seeing, questions of occupation and space, the position and relevance of the so-called 'lyrical I', and conditions of referentiality. My work may be symptomatic of late modernism (even post-modernism) in its exploration of the processes of its own creation and investigation of language as a thing-in-itself, but its concerns are primarily ethical and moral in nature. Visual art is a strong inspiration.

JOHN KINSELLA

Plumburst

for Wendy

The neat greens of Monument Hill
roll into sea, over the rise the soft rain
of plumfall deceives us in its groundburst.

If lightning strikes from the ground up,
and Heaven is but an irritation that prompts
its angry spark, then plums are born
dishevelled on the ground and rise
towards perfection ...

Out of the range of rising plums
we mark the territory of the garden,
testing caprock with Judas trees,
pacing out melon runs. Behind us a block
of flats hums into dusk and the sun
bursts a plum mid-flight.

Pig Melons

As children we dashed
their brains out,
the insipid flesh
drying like chunks of pork
over the yellowing paddocks;
this murder bringing
further ruin to arable lands,
choking the native flora
with spilt thoughts
encoded as seeds
that bided their time
spitefully
until the rains

washed away the tracks
of our games, our conflicts,
percolating beneath the surface,
throwing ropes
that crept out,
securing the meagre
fertility of the place
with their rituals
of bondage.

Skeleton weed / generative grammar

for Noam Chomsky

(I) Finite-state

The 'i' takes in what is said —
yes, it is easily led
across the floors of discourse
only to find itself a force
easily reckoned with: there's
no point in stock-taking arrears
as fleshly interests tell you
nothing except acceptability & taboo.
Take skeleton weed infesting
the crop — rosette of basal
leaves unleashing a fatal
stem with daisy-like flowers
that drop (into) parachute clusters
of seeds. One missed when
they scour the field (men
& women anonymously clothed
seated on a spidery raft dragged
behind a plodding tractor,
monotony testing the free-will factor),
can lead to disaster.

(ii) Phrase-structure

{[((analyz)ing)] [the ((constituent)s]}
we examine (?) the wool of sheep
for free-loading skeleton-weed seeds,
their teeth specifically designed
for wool: the ag department
have decided they ARE selective
though admit our investigations
will help their 'research'.

(iii) transformational

One year the farmer asked us if we
felt guilty for missing one & hence ruining
his would-have-been bumper crop.
Quarantined the following year. Losing
his unseeded would-be bumper crop.
Ruining his credit rating. His marriage.
His son's & daughter's places
at their exclusive city boarding
schools. His problem with alcohol.
His subsequent breakdown
& hospitalization. (?) We remained
& still remain passive. We still remain
& remained passive. Still we remained
& remain passive. But we [look(ed)] deeply,
collectively & independently
into our SELVES. Our silence
was an utterance of a loud inner speech.
A loud inner speech was an utterance
of our silence. Speaking for myself,
I've included in my lexicon of guilt
the following: what I feel today
will I feel tomorrow? And those tight
yellow flowers: so beautiful on the wiry
structures they call 'skeleton weed'.

Rat Tunnels in the Wall of the Horse Dam

Like monks tunnelling into desert
mesas, a vibrant hermitage surrounded
by a moat of sand, rats have tunnelled
deep into the walls of the horse dam.

But their science is flawed — it's Autumn
now and the rains have yet to come,
Summer lies low in the hollowed ground,
a brackish indolent puddle — Winter

will unleash the flood that will fill
the lowest chambers, drive rats with young
blindly towards the upper galleries,
as frenzied as victims in disaster films

who've realised technology is just a mask
to hide a human failing — 'we can't be wrong,
we've considered every alternative'. But God
makes kingdoms in the strangest places.

Warhol at Wheatlands

He's polite looking over the polaroids
saying gee & fantastic, though always
standing close to the warm glow

of the Wonderheat as the flames
lick the self-cleansing glass.
It's winter down here & the sudden

change has left him wanting. Fog
creeps up from the gullies & toupées
the thinly pastured soil. It doesn't

remind him of America at all. But there's
a show on television about New York so
we stare silently, maybe he's asleep

behind his dark glasses? Wish Tom
& Nicole were here. He likes the laser
prints of Venice cluttering the hallway,

the sun a luminous patch trying
to break through the dank cotton air
& the security film on the windows.

Deadlocks & hardened glass make him feel
comfortable, though being locked inside
with Winchester rifles has him tinfoiling

his bedroom — he asks one of us but we're
getting ready for seeding & can't spare a moment.
Ring-necked parrots sit in the fruit trees

& he asks if they're famous. But he
doesn't talk much (really). Asked about Marilyn
he shuffles uncomfortably — outside, in the

spaces between parrots & fruit trees
the stubble rots & the day fails
        to sparkle.

Jackknife

The back end catching up
& skewing shockingly
across the hitching pin,
jagging sideways and cracking
the spine of the truck,
the trailer arse-up & the driver
shot through the windscreen
over the bullbar, his load
of sheep ground into a rough
slurry, minced through the grilles,
the asphalt a rink filled
with a greasy slick of blood
on which tailing vehicles
slide into the grotesque
haute couture of metal
and Pure New Wool — a pile-up
on the Interstate Highway,
an epistemological
wreckage.

ANTHONY LAWRENCE

To speak with knowledge and clarity about style and the direction my poetry is taking has never been easy. The reader has a far better chance at defining this territory. My influences are another matter. I read constantly and widely, from beginning writers to celebrated poets. Reading poetry helps in two distinct ways: it keeps me in touch with what's happening around the world, and it feeds my own work. There's nothing like the flare inside a poem to make you want to sit down and start/return to writing.

For years I've been called a narrative poet. This might be so. I like telling stories within the boundaries of a poem, be it over two or thirty pages. I also like to refine and burnish. Lyrical poetry has a different breath and afterglow. When I've successfully combined a narrative and lyrical vein, I'm amazed. A spell has been woven and broken. In my forthcoming book *The Crow is Not a Piper*, I have maintained my love of the longer, musical line, while experimenting with a variety of new forms. It's an exciting consolidation and departure.

Fencing

High tensile wire, when strained,
is a volatile thing.
I'd been warned how the wire can break,
whipping back through the eyes
of the fence posts, leaving your fingers
flexing at your feet, or worse,
your throat smiling redly from ear to ear.
You hear stories.

I was straining the last section before smoko.
I worked the handle of the strainer back and forth,
daydreaming, watching clouds move in.
Then I heard it: a loud ping like a struck tuning fork.
I leapt away from the fence as the wire
ripped past me — silver, on fire,
with my name cut into its tail.

Whistling Fox

My father could whistle up a fox
with the bent lid of a jam tin.
Pursing his lips, he would blow the cries
of a wounded hare into cold Glen Innes hills.
Into a giant's marble game of balancing granite;
the wind-peeled stones on the tablelands
of New England; a sound like a child
crying called the fox from its nest of skin and bones.

I was there the day my father blew
the eyes from a small red fox.
He fired, opened the shotgun over his knee,
and handed me two smoking shells.

201

It had come to us like any whistled dog,
leaving its padmarks in frosty grass.
That day it left its winter coat behind
with blood like rubies sown into the dripping hem.

A Most Troublesome Possession

One thousand miles, the landscape predictable
and contained as in a sandbox diorama,
the highway's vanishing-point painted
onto cardboard backing, mirage-flooded
at the summit and planted with grey sticks
for poles — the bush telegraph wired against
a big sun suspended over northwest mining towns.
As I drive, the sky discharges insects like shot
from a sawn-off scatter gun, the windshield
a slaughterman's visor — then, as I crest
a bald rise near the Overlander roadhouse,
the magnified face of James Dickey
looming through a squall of warm Korean rain,
one eye closed for greater accuracy,
the other open though glazed over with communist
blood and flaksmoke. How such visions manifest
themselves is a cruel mystery — no more
disturbing image have I entertained, especially
when considering the extensive necrology
of Australian road travel. I tried to anticipate
Dickey's response to the carnage: would he
pause to comment sadly on the lines
of kangaroos lying stiff-limbed like exhausted
travellers under brown coats on the verge,
or would his approval be rapturous and long-
winded over such a display — ripe potential
for working poetry from the death of animals?
He offered no response, preferring to maintain
a low and tight-lipped altitude. So I hit
the coast road trying to shake him, and found

Kalbarri calm with pensioners taking the sun,
melting long slivers of ice from their bones.
I got out for air and found the poet unhitching
his face from the dusty trailer of my wake.
Before I could speak, he entered the water
and went out past the lines of breakers,
his great ruddy head going under like Easter
Island stone. I saw him offering directions
to a stalled cavalcade of rainbow-scaled reef dwellers
wafting south on the Leeuwin current,
bearing aloft like seaweed the tattered remains
of a child who'd gone overboard off Exmouth
during a light-tackle gamefish tournament.
Her parents were still sending up flares
from the dunes and combing the shorebreak
for her clothes, for anything that would provide
some proof of her existence in the world.
Dickey offered the child his blessing, his tears
licked away by an attendance of small blue eels.
When he climbed from the foam he recited
'The Performance' haltingly through a mouthful
of shells and sand, as if trying to make
some connection between his headless friend
and the child whose death he'd only just mourned.
The shadow of a touring cloud fell upon him
and he was gone, his face and voice entering
my eyes and moving there like great poetry.
Then I was driving again, and as if to ease
the burden of such a wild and troublesome
possession, a scattering of Port Lincoln parrots
wearing collars of black feathers came loudly
over the road — spears of green light shrieking
away into the trees. I drove, and the sky let
down its colours. And somewhere outside Cataby,
something like a Tasmanian Tiger was tearing
at itself, doubled over in a saltbush at the roadside.
I expected James Dickey to reappear, to kneel
beside the animal and question it on the nature
of pain and extinction. But nothing emerged
from the cloud of dust and flies the creature
was writhing under, its muscled flanks veined
blackly with tyre burns. And then a blowout

doing ninety, almost hammered to scrap metal
by a wheat truck, the driver's finger out the window
carving *fuck you* in the air —
torn rubber melting over the handle of the jack,
my spit fizzing like eggwhite on hot gravel
beside the flattened body of a bobtail lizard,
its blue tongue rolled out thick with jumping ants.
Outside Yanchep, wildflowers lit the spaces
between gums locking into each other, making
a twisted canopy, though some were bleached
and falling, rattled with dieback, flushed
with salt, or whatever it is the root systems
of the west have been drinking from earth
infected by grubs, mismanagement or chemicals.
Fourteen hours from Carnarvon to Perth,
the huge Capricorn skies diminishing the further
south you drive. No music. No talk. The surreal
attentions of an American poet and the legacy
of his company: a passenger seat ablaze
with purple flowers — pickings from a walk
through fields of Paterson's Curse — the bees
in my hair, droning like Dickey's farewell
reminder: *Be sure to utilize the skin, bones*
and organs of everything you see, and remember,
no landscape, no outcome is predictable.
I stop at a Swan Valley vineyard and throw back
tumblers of claret at a tasting. I buy three
bottles, open one, and slug dry vintage
recklessly as I go, market gardens becoming
the outer suburbs, the late sun caught redly
in a tilted bottleneck. Half pissed by the time
I roar into Fremantle, a few surfers paddling in dusklight,
the poetry of a long drive on the make,
the engine killed, and the last bottle
drained off like communion in a carpark
overlooking the sea.

The Mercenary Heart

An American poet, walking on a farm outside
Carson City, Nevada, found blue feathers
and bones caught in fence wire.

Perhaps it was because she knew her native birds
so well, or because what she found inflamed
a need to record her own fragmented life.

Whatever the reasons, she reconstructed
the death of a great blue heron
from the moment it left the nest to the time

the wind chained it thrashing to the barbs.
For my part, I'm indifferent to the bird's death —
to what happened between its low flying

through Nevada farms, its arrival at the wire,
and how it looked when the poet
chanced upon its remains. What really gets me

is that I can read her poem, take what I need,
then write something worth preserving of my own,
completely ignorant of America's native birds

and the poets that use them, alive or dead,
for inspiration. I've seen the bristling
crucifixions of eagles on Australian farms —

feathers, talons, and straw-thin bones
stitched against the wind like a curse
that rarely fulfills its black intentions.

And I've considered, in passing them,
using their flightless warnings to fire
the poetry I promised myself I'd write one day —

words like bones, gathered and assembled
into the myths their various functions
have invented out of air. My reasons

for writing this are difficult to explain,
that is if there are any reasons at all.
Though, as with the American poet

(Blue Heron Death as therapy, a theme
lifted from the wire), the warnings have gone
unheeded, and the poem has made it through,

knowing any action can be used
and justified when the mercenary heart
has been out hunting once again.

Dugite Skeletons

An expired Catherine wheel of segmented bones on a limestone cliff overlooking the beach on Bernier Island, in the Indian Ocean. Bernier and Dorre Islands were used by Jonathan Swift for Brobdingnag and Lilliput. He lifted them from Dirck Hartog's maps.

Dugites position themselves for death in exposed places, usually with the head facing North.

On Dorre Island, dugite skeletons have been violated, the bones disconnected then replaced a few centimetres apart, thus giving the appearance of much bigger reptiles. The fangs had been removed. The heads pointed East.

Dirck Hartog had a tattoo of a dugite skeleton coiling around his left shoulder.

Jonathan Swift made no mention of snakes, or their skeletons in *Gulliver's Travels*, despite there being an elaborate border of reptile bones around the borders of Hartog's maps.

If you find a dugite skeleton on a small, sub-tropical island or in the mainland bush, kneel and place your ear above the centre of the bone spiral. Hold your breath. Soon you'll hear the spent cries of small marsupials, also the sound of venom claiming the miniature networks of their veins.

RHYLL McMASTER

My poems reflect subjective feelings and objective observations, but increasingly I am interested in how we have those feelings and why we believe our observations are objective. Does the world exist or only when we are looking at it?

Why do we come up with concepts such as the soul and why do so many intelligent people believe in angels and gods?

Science is self-renewing like the Magic Pudding, because though it works by setting up theoretical propositions as answers to questions, it seems it will never answer the question of the mystery of the existence of consciousness of the questioner.

We are 'in some state/beyond crystalline command' but how do we explain the brain state of desire?

Clever

I doubt that an axe-cleft
through the centre
of my mother's forehead
would change her expressions
of wistful envy —
'Such a talented girl and her daughters
went to school X'.
Stroke follows stroke like thunderstorms
that keep circling back,
yet she still finds the words —
'One's now a clever doctor,
one's a clever clever'.
She stops, snaps and sucks at her food,
good manners dropped.
'The youngest did something very clever'.

She does not notice
she is clinging to the inside
of a dark tin drum.
She can't feel herself suspended in space.
She expends all her energy
hanging on.

Flying The Coop

When death approaches
the faint hum
of the body disappears,
the way the fan in the freezer space
cuts out as you reach for the ice-tray
quietly but unambiguously
the suddenness of inaction
implacable absence,

the leave taking
that doesn't take long
the walking off
without drawn-out explanations.

When death approached me
I felt levitated with fever.
I was in an oil-filled capsule,
my snug hospital bed.
I did not tell anyone I was dying
or not for a while.
I let myself die a bit.
I sank down.
I was never so relaxed
comatose as a scarab grub
in the ruby glow of dirt-underground.

It was as if the ultimate fusion
had occurred on my father's lap,
my armpit to his chest
my cheek to the curve of his neck.
Death cuddled me, detached
and read a book
smelling of cigarettes and whisky.

Death was bottomless
as the black basalt swimming hole
above Nerang
but without the fear of cold.
It was warm as a rock pool
late afternoon on Snapper Rocks.

Death shaped me like an ear,
curled up, cleaned out as a dried apricot
waiting for the tongue
of something like a mouth
someone like a god.

Sea Creatures

I am terrified
out in the lime juice sea
bobbing next to my father beyond the sand bar
in open ocean.

He grins down at me
his teeth strong and yellow
with brown nicotined edges.
Out of my depth,
waves cracking like broken glass,
I paddle doggedly.

I am afraid of what I can't see,
of jellyfish and drowning,
of being dumped by punches of water.
I can't measure up.
My father vaults serene.

I am underneath green, deserted, round-edged water
in a whirl of curtained sand.
I reach the beach — the world is still
staggeringly the same.
There's my mother sitting like a capped sponge.

She smiles slightly in her black togs.
She is round in sections
like hard dough buns.
Her metal zipper is the green of verdigris.
She looks astonished at her contained capacity.

My mother enters the water ceremoniously.
She corks perpendicularly beneath her bathing cap.
Her round head sits on her round bosoms

which balance on her round stomach
like a black and rotund peach.
She glistens like a sea cow, she wallows.
She allows the water to wash over her.

Emerging, she dries consideringly
in a juddering towel huddle.
Off with her chin-strapped cap, herself again
and her perm springs free.

I dash back into the water.
It is a torture.
It fights me with a slap.
I have sand in my teeth.
Something brushes my leg.
Sea lice bite.
My eyes, red-rimmed, sting.
In the will of the moment I believe
I am having dreadful fun.

Company Man

Isaac Newton hugged his inventions,
paper lovers, close to his chest.
Dad didn't.
He handed them over at the Company's behest.

The Company gave him a car,
a Humber Snipe,
the Company gave him a reason for life.
Mum didn't.

The Company loved him.
So did Mum.
But the Company squeezed his heart in a vice,
it was faithless.
It winked and capered.

Dad lugged his soul that the Company bent
to the side of the grave, a short dark bed.
'I feel crook', he said
and lumbered in.

Mum said,
'They've been good to us
considering'.

Night Etiquette

Don't hog the bed, dog/man.
Be aligned with grace.
You lie fallow
burning and glowering
like a smouldering log.
Stretch light in bed.

Where are your nighttime manners?
You turn your face aside,
growl, heavily sigh,
expending bad air.
Your dreams snag,
taking up space in my peace of mind.

Half those sheets you shrug away are mine.
Those coverings also cover me.
Hours of our eternity
spent gloomily side by side, sick animals.
Your back's landscape a sandbag
and looming, the strange boulder of your head.

Receptacle

Once I was a bin
with one thing in it:
a glaring light from out there;
white, fizzing particles.

I gave in, aced by my first delight.
I had no lid,
no resistance.
I abnegated my right
to say when was garbage night,
to say divulge or enclose
or hey, what's that
so tightly wrapped?
Wait a minute!

When I grew wheels,
scooting round the garden,
filled myself with dark air,
blue pegs, bits of refracting tin
and a deep, viscous substance,
I became dangerous:
no bin can be autonomous.

An unbiddable bin
is a doomed bin,
just begging to be replaced
by a stationary bin,
with no arms, no legs
no face.

JENNIFER MAIDEN

I write to solve the problem of evil. As I age, this becomes clearer and clearer to me. This might appear to insult the current taste for helpless microcosms and lovely lyrical details and writers of great humility, but such microcosms trouble me deeply. An editor told me that I write as if I was re-inventing the language, but that is because re-inventing the language is still a moral necessity if we are to escape the rigid cultural, linguistic and biological microcosms which result in violence. It seems to me that one of the main manifestations of the problem of evil is the uncritical hierarchization of roles, accompanied by an unstable, insatiable urge for hierarchization — whether they need to be at the top or bottom — in people who have suffered the violence *of* hierarchization. I think the solution is not an impossible equality but rather a situation of deliberate and fluxing role-reversal, such as that present in art and sex. Writing not only allows one to practise such continuous writer/reader reversals of power, but to explore these reversals in the macrocosmal context — how they work or could work in life. Therefore, despite its preoccupation with terrible examples of evil, my work is also meant to be conceptually expansive and concisely celebratory in style. Working through a difficult computer program, my daughter asked me to stay in the room, because she might need me as 'a witness to triumph', and that felt like a good thing to be.

'Can We Dive Into The Monster, Jenny?'

On my verandah,
                I am sipping lemongrass
tea.   At the Powerhouse Special Effects
display, the kids from Katharine's
then-school were on another planet, about
to be devoured by a centipede the size
of a dinosaur when one of them on the stage,
which was actually bare (the monster
being only on the screen) called out, 'Can we
dive into the monster, Jenny?', playing. Later,
maybe they did dive in, because they bullied
my daughter without mercy that she
and a friend featured often on a Powerhouse
rock video when in fact all the others
had refused their next turns with an air displaying
experienced boredom.   A little thing, maybe,
but she sat immobile,
               white to the soul with pain, she
who was too experienced
for boredom, and who had never
seen herself on video before. I had the courage
to strategically over-react and take
her away from the school.   Also,
at the Powerhouse I learned that Oscar
de la Renta perfume (my favourite) is based on Guerlain's
L'Heure Bleue which uses lemongrass, and that
the electric chair was invented to be
painless but that it really simultaneously
fries, paralyses and suffocates its victims, who
stay conscious quite a long time. They had
a real electric chair there (so small). My
husband sat down on it, playing, maybe
not knowing what it was. I was
the reader of fine print always, asked
him to vacate the monster. In the 1920s
an American woman who killed her husband
(I saw on CNN) died in the chair, was photographed
illegally during the process and published on
the front page of a paper under

the headline 'DEAD!'. But of course
at that stage she probably wasn't. The photo
showed petticoat, legs and gappy eyes, a dreadful
rigid stillness.   One problem
of evil is when to expect it, how to slow
that expectation into sips,
                        small enough to allow
withdrawal or confrontation. On my verandah
here, therefore, this lemongrass
tea I have invented to spare you
too much abstract logic smells
authentically of dread and de la Renta.

The Case Of The Dalmatian Diamond

                        It's been a black and white week.
I bought a 1.03 carat diamond, craving to
wear that much purity on my hand, but
affordable one carats have inclusions
and so does this one, under the glass:
a tiny black planet with moons. So
I joked about 'Spotty the Diamond', at
last trying out Sherlock Holmes titles:
'A Diamond in Dalmatia', or at best
'The Dalmatian Diamond', since my child
is into Disney Dalmatians and bought
one at the Show, spread out on
its belly, like Miss O'Murphy, that
cheerful Boucher courtesan. It is also
the anniversary of U.S. withdrawal
from Vietnam and my satellite receiver
has an extra transponder for Ho
Chi Minh City. While I work, my peripheral
vision picks it up. On the rooftop of the former
U.S. Embassy, Robert Wiener, the
CNN Producer, and Peter Arnett clown between
standups. CNN proper recalls Arnett's Pulitzer

for reporting the U.S. disaster
in Vietnam.   In daylight, that roof
is clear as a dawn diamond, but
at night has tricky shadow. Off
camera, Wiener worries, 'It looks like
a night-shot in the middle of Baghdad
during the war. I really think this fucking
roof only works in daytime'. Later,
on CNN proper, the present Administrator
of Kent State University says that
students at Kent State 'learned their lesson'
from being shot dead during Vietnam, and when
the Gulf War happened didn't protest so
extremely as they once did. No,
indeed. On a discussion program, Arnett
mentions that the final Gulf War footage
was censored utterly by the Media, not
because it was grisly or saturating but
for political reasons. He doesn't go
into what or why. Spinning the dial
between transponders, I find the Bob Dylan
'Unplugged' concert. He sings in Japanese
PAL colour, his diction improved
vastly since the Sixties and his emphasis
better, I think. He concludes with 'If
God's on *our* side, he will stop the next
war', and I like the new italics. I feel
a relief of communion with my husband, also
accidentally enthralled by this better-
than-nostalgia. I'm grateful to myself
that, at seventeen, I went on record in
the *Australian* to contradict Knopfelmacher
and Evan Jones. I argued that George Orwell
was a socialist and would have thought Vietnam
was wrong. My husband describes his march
in the Moratorium. Back on the Ho Chi Minh
transponder, Arnett's in the night street
like Hester in *The Scarlet Letter*. For an hour
before crowds, he stands, alternately
jocular, nervous or angered at
'amateurish crap' in on-air linkage. Behind
him somewhere a Viet rock gig celebrates

217

war's end more than winning it, the dense
bright chiaroscuro street, the faces.
As a child escaping home, I kept
a commonplace book called *The Terms*
in which I quoted Kelen the artist:
that the smiling face has such beauty, why
would anyone want to stop that? Another
quote, which once helped me with the death
of my father, was Huxley's on re-marriage:
'The best monument to tenderness is
tenderness'.   The poem
I wrote last week is about the need
for explorative words in grief, but a friend
hearing it insists gently that
on her mother's death no words could help.
but that *is* words, of course, although I don't
argue too much: disloyalty to
the dead is a delicate matter, and
my poem began with the empty beds
in another room (that time they were
of Oklahoma children). Chiaroscuro
has always seemed to me to be
an existential pattern. On a transponder,
a U.S. marine recounts how an old man
offered him a bag of uncut diamonds
if he'd airlift his family away, but he
had to return it, refuse. Flicked through
PAL and NTSC, the transponders turn
black and white at last.   Early
in my work I wrote a 'cow poem' on
Friesians in which their hide became
a simile for life and death. My daughter and I
joke about 'black and white cutes', and
she won a panda on the Show Clowns, wrote
'I felt as if I had won a diamond'. She brought
home a toy Friesian from the milk
exhibit. My new diamond has a milky
glitter, reminds me of Wallace Stevens: 'When
the thinking of God is smoky dew'. For
my daughter's ninth birthday, I suggest
a rock 'n' roll party. Would Dylan sound new?
The diamond is set in tight, old-fashioned

claws, is as clear and concentric as
a Georgia O'Keeffe lily. The US transponders
are full of Robert McNamara
humbly answering critics, some
of whom lost families, bits
of bodies and brains, about why
he knows now the Domino Theory
was wrong. I think: how black and white
and subliminal a domino is, that my hair
glints black and white now. On a transponder
behind Arnett at my eye's corner, night
burns like a diamond in Saigon.

'Look, I'm standing on no-floor'

            said Margaret Cunningham's four-
year-old daughter Tessa, her fingers
clenched whitely on the table-edge, her feet
luxuriously in air. Margaret is still Director
of STARTTS, the NSW Service for Torture
and Trauma Rehab., and I am still their
sort of Writer-on-Call. Together
we wrote a chapter about a child
called Layla who comes from no-country
in particular, a fact which has already —
together with the letterhead Torture and Trauma —
put off at least one publisher. Layla
has witnessed torture and many other
forms of not-belonging. Margaret and I often
have also stood on no-floor, child or woman.
                        After Tessa
said that, I joked about the shoes
I'd worn the day before: open high-heels
very black and very tall, and very
precarious: 'I was standing on no-floor
a lot yesterday', but it was
worth it because I only paid nine

219

dollars for the sandals and felt as sexy
as something airy from another world.
                              But the torture:
Margaret joked about a phone call
to the T & T unit from the cloistered ABC,
asking to interview clients who'd really
enjoyed their torture, were into S-M. I
observed this was a travesty of my theory
that people after trauma need a hierarchy
but both idealise and demonise it, and that
recognition of S-M in their sexuality
might clarify this process for them:
                              hell,
when you're standing on no-floor, you skate
or fall or just stay-put, appreciate
the elevation. We also spoke of Arthur
Stieglitz photographing Georgia O'Keeffe
as hundreds of nudes, and how women at one
of Margaret's workshops had gone out to pay
a photographer to give them back their bodies.
One works better in all areas, I think, with
a confidence in one's geography,
                              and if
there's a vaginal velvet emptiness at centre
studded with that vaginal
                              diamond mine of nerves,
no-floor is not a life-defining problem.
                              On the wall
near this table at Margaret's, a Georgia
O'Keeffe lily is as poised as Tessa's joy.

PETER MINTER

Broadly speaking, my work applies contemporary frames to significant issues in Australian poetry. This is carried out by synchronising two related formal approaches to composition. Firstly, I write poetry which takes the idea of 'landscape' and its representation as a central point of reference. This work explores and experiments with many narratorial and lyrical elements, most of which will be familiar to readers of Australian poetry. However, far from simple reiteration, I hope to reinvigorate these forms by applying contemporary notions of language as a material and cultural object. By creating ground from which current trends in poetics will continue to inform Australia poetry into the next century, these poems carry forward one of the tasks taken up by the 'Generation of '68', who in various ways squared off and dealt with the semantic and ontological gulf they found between language and the environment.

Secondly, my current work looks to a selection of Australian poetry texts and 'rewrites' them, thereby using the poems themselves as a reference point rather than 'the landscape'. Keeping the concept of the palimpsest as a figuring device, I attempt to re- or over-write older works, most of which would be considered canonical, and attempt to use them as a point of contact between the history of Australian poetry, its ideas and aesthetics, and new ways of perceiving and acting in the world as a writer. In a sense, these new poems work in dialogue with the originals, drawing on similar geographic locations, thematic devices and language forms, while also drawing them forward to participate in the creation of a contemporary poetic informed by international trends in Language, hybridised and prose poetries.

Palimpsestina: Monument To Banks

There is no comparison
between puffer fish and hollow
effigies of skin, the dry just holding
phonemes, teeth, shadows
in the socket where an eye
spoke, presence indefinite

as morphemes, indefinite
like scales compared to the nose
of a botanist, Linnaean, eyeing
decay from a bronze hollow,
the shadow of 'Cock' resilient
as spray paint held on the monument's

side. Nature takes monumental
umbrage, suspicious of metaphor or shade,
a carcass or two shrunk on the lawn
by the waves. Smelling of inconsistency,
rust, your lunch is wasted
by knowledge, sensuality, vision

of a hard beak, a puffer fish's brow
and rows of spikes, teeth unnaturally
on the grass beside you, scraps
of foliage and bones singing in a hot
breeze, your scientist friend insisting
on precedence, bloated with interpreting grass.

Where settlement becomes thick reeds
spoiling the method of his gaze
a 7-Up bottle floats down stream, resisting
gravity and description like a prenatal
republican cap, rousing whitebait, heat
blistering the plastic skin into air traps

winding over smaller fish trapped
lank beneath lines and bristling reeds
busy as strophes with the burnt
horror of revision, unable to fix or see

a puffer fish hardening out of nature
as he falls again into vectors, waits, then sinks.

Tornado

Un amico dell'acqua, or so you saw him,
trapped in reeds and, naturally excited,
moulding, steaming speechlessness.

Ruin'd Cottage

Difference the story makes telling
The story makes a difference your
Story is you make your history making
The hero of the story making history

a.

Still interrupted
An exchange happens in *the now*
Brought about by a story with problems
Of closure to do with *the know*,
A transition between ending and coming in,
Saying that good bye.

The he of the poem is very touched.
We are not told what he says,
Just words in transition. The curtain
Comes down quickly,
The blind, the difficulty of closure.

b.

The first person, the old one
The pedlar variously
Named as fragmentary parts
Of displaced Wordsworthian selves,
An autobiographical. Relate it,
Placed close to. If your narrator
is an old man
He has a long grey beard, pointed.
Experience has aged him,
Made him wary.

(she can't tell her own story,
she had no wish to live
that she must die of sorrow).

c.

It was to be titled: thus.
We die my friend, peculiar
Nooks of earth. And senseless rocks.

Etcetera. Etcetera.
Won't go on any longer;
The story itself is so closely linked:
experiences and Telling it
will happen when he tells it,
Who he chooses to tell it to
Obedient to the strong creative will
Of human passion.

d.

Well, love, of course. Does love?
Is suffering, passion will the voice?

The still and the sad. These stories are
The stories of the deaths of children,

Take your pick, sword or fever, accident or neglect.
Or indiscretion, a tale winding up

The voice, the primary trope,
An oral art that writing speaks.

The fuel is human passion.
Lines forty-nine, onwards,

The voice of human passion.
Lyrical eloquence released

By loss has its origin in the death
Of somebody else. No death, no elegy,

No audible evidence. By grace
And the christian religion, every elegy

is the voice of the strong, divine
Redemption reclaiming an eloquence

A sacrifice
Of women, the children.

e.

He had become an unemployed weaver,
The husband, a victim before that last ditched
Chance to go off and be killed.

Cut off by the season, enclosure,
And on top of this comes a war,
All heaped up, which claims the necessary

Sacrifice and has empowered also
Poetry! The double dimension and,
On the other hand, the sacrifice.

f.

And to find his voice, if
We draw attention to the joints

In narrative, to a story moreover,
Which covers a slice of recent misery

In the five years past, a crucial five
When war broke out. And a tale of woe

Appalled and aghast at this duplicity.

Expose the mechanism and go past
The mechanism, past genre, find a way

Between elegy, history, perhaps.
Its not, its narrative. This awkward point,

Where sublime loss
Comes suddenly

Unstuck from the sequence of events.

LES MURRAY

Art is indefensible.

Water-Gardening in an Old Farm Dam

Blueing the blackened water
that I'm widening with my spade
as I lever up water tussocks
and chuck them ashore like sopping comets
is a sun-point, dazzling heatless
acetylene, under tadpoles that swarm
wobbling, like a species of flies
and buzzing bubbles that speed
upward like many winged species.

Unwettable green tacos are lotus leaves
Waterlily leaves are notched plaques
of the water. Their tubers resemble
charred monstera trunks. Some I planted,
some I let float. And I bought
thumb-sized mosquito-eating fish
for a dollar in a plastic amnion.
'Wilderness' says we've lost belief
in human building: our dominance
now so complete that we hide it.

Where, with my levered back,
I stand, too late in life,
in a populous amber, feet deep
in digesting chyle over clays,
I love green humanised water
in old brick pounds, water carried
unleaking for miles around contour,
or built out into, or overstepping
stonework in long frilled excess.

The hands' pride and abysmal
pay that such labour earned,
as against the necks and billions
paid for Nature. But the workers
and the need are gone, without reaching
here: this was never canal country.
It's cow-ceramic, softened at rain times,
where the kookaburra's laugh
is like angles of a scrubbing toothbrush
heard through the bones of the head.

Level water should turn out of sight,
on round a bend, behind an island,
in windings of possibility, not
be exhausted in one gesture, like an avenue.
It shouldn't be surveyable in one look.
That's a waterhole. Still, the trees
I planted along this one bend it
a bit, and half roof it, bringing
its wet underearth shadow to the surface
as shade. And the reeds I hate,

mint sheaves, human-high palisades
that would close in round the water,
I could fire floating petrol among them
again, and savage but not beat them,
or I could declare them beautiful.

Blowfly Grass

The houses those suburbs could afford
were roofed with old savings books, and some
seeped gravy at stiches in their walls;

some were clipped as close as fury,
some grimed and corner-bashed by love
and the real estate, as it got more vacant

grew blady grass and blowfly grass, so called
for the exquisite lanterns of its seed
and the land sagged subtly to a low point,

it all inclined way out there to a pit
with burnt-looking cheap marble edges
and things and figures flew up from it

like the stones in the crusher Piers had
for making dusts of them for glazes:
flint, pyroclase, slickensides, quartz, schist,

snapping, refusing and spitting high
till the steel teeth got gritty corners on them
and could grip them craw-chokingly to grind.

It's their chance, a man with beerglass-cut arms
told me. Those hoppers got to keep filled. A girl,
edging in, bounced out cropped and wrong-coloured.

like a chemist's photo crying. Who could blame her
among in-depth grabs and Bali flights and phones?
She was true, and got what truth gets.

Little Boy Impelling A Scooter

Little boy on a wet pavement
near nightfall, balancing his scooter,
his free foot spurring it along,
his every speeding touchdown
striking a match of spent light,
the long concrete patched with squeezed-dry impacts
coming and going, his tyres' rubber edge
splitting the fine water. He jinks the handlebars
and trots around them, turning them
back, and stamps fresh small impulsions
maddeningly on and near, off and behind
his earlier impulses.
                    Void blurring pavement stars,
void blurring wheel-noise, uneven with hemmed outsets
as the dark deepens over town. To bear his rapture,
to smile, to share in it, require attitudes
all remote from murder,
watching his bowed intent face and slackly trailing
sudden pump leg passing and hemm! repassing
under powerlines and windy leaves
and the bared night sky's interminable splendours.

Second Essay on Interest: the Emu

Weathered blond as a grass tree, a huge Beatles haircut
raises an alert periscope and stares out
over scrub. Her large olivine eggs click
oilily together; her lips of noble plastic
clamped in their expression, her head-fluff a stripe
worn mohawk style, she bubbles her pale-blue windpipe:
the emu, *Dromaius novaehollandiae,*
whose stand-in on most continents is an antelope,
looks us in both eyes with her one eye
and her other eye, dignified courageous hump,
feather-swaying condensed camel, Swift Courser of New Holland.

Knees backward in toothed three-way boots you stand,
Dinewan, proud emu, common as the dust
in your sleeveless cloak, returning our interest.
Your shield of fashion's wobbly: you're Quaint, you're Native,
even somewhat Bygone. You may be let live
but beware: the blank zones of Serious disdain
are often carte blanche to the darkly human.
Europe's boats on their first strange shore looked humble
but, Mass over, men started renaming the creatures.
Worship turned to interest and had new features.
Now only life survives, if it's made remarkable.

Heraldic bird, our protection is a fable
made of space and neglect. We're remarkable and not;
we're the ordinary discovered on a strange planet.
Are you Early or Late, in the history of birds
which doesn't exist, and is deeply ancient?
My kinships too, are immemorial and recent,
like my country, which abstracts yours in words.
This distillate of mountains is finely branched, this plain
expanse of dour delicate lives, where the rain,
shrouded slab on the west horizon, is a corrugated revenant
settling its long clay-tipped plumage in a hatching descent.

Rubberneck, stepped sister, I see your eye on our jeep's load.
I think your story is, when you were offered
the hand of evolution, you gulped it. Forefinger and thumb

project from your face, but the weighing palm is inside you
collecting the bottletops, nails, wet cement that you famously swallow,
your passing muffled show, your serially private museum.
Some truths are now called *trivial*, though. Only God approves them.
Some humans who disdain them make a kind of weather
which, when it grows overt and widespread, we call *war*.
There we make death trivial and awesome, by rapid turns about,
we conscript it to bless us, force-feed it to squeeze the drama out;

indeed we imprison and torture death — this part is called peace —
we offer it murder like mendicants, begging for significance.
You rustle dreams of pardon, not fleeing in your hovercraft style
not gliding fast with zinc-flaked legs dangling, feet making high-tensile
seesawing impacts. Wasteland parent, barely edible dignitary,
the disinterested spotlight of the lords of interest
and gowned nobles of ennui is a torch of vivid arrest
and blinding after-darkness. But you hint it's a brigand sovereignty
after the steady extents of God's common immortality
whose image is daylight detail, aggregate, in process yet plumb
to the everywhere focus of one devoid of boredom.

Bats' Ultrasound

Sleeping-bagged in a duplex wing
with fleas, in rock-cleft or building
radar bats are darkness in miniature,
their whole face one tufty crinkled ear
with weak eyes, fine teeth bared to sing.

Few are vampires. None flit through the mirror.
Where they flutter at evening's a queer
tonal hunting zone above highest C.
Insect prey at the peak of our hearing
drone re to their detailing tee:

ah, eyrie-ire, aero hour, eh?
O'er our ur-area (our era aye
ere your raw row) we air our array,
err, yaw, row wry — aura our orrery,
our eerie ü our ray, our arrow.

A rare ear, our aery Yahweh.

One Kneeling, One Looking Down

Half-buried timbers chained corduroy
lead out into the sand
which bare feet wincing Crutch and Crotch
spurn for the summer surf's embroidery
and insects stay up on the land.

A storm engrossing half the sky
in broccoli and seething drab
and standing on one foot over the country
burrs like a lit torch. Lightning
turns air to elixir at every grab

but the ocean sky is untroubled blue
everywhere. Its storm rolls below:
sand clouds raining on sacred country
drowned a hundred lifetimes under sea.
In the ruins of a hill, channels flow,

and people, like a scant palisade
driven in the surf, jump or sway
or drag its white netting to the tide line
where a big man lies with his limbs splayed,
fingers and toes and a forehead-shine

as if he'd fallen off the flag.
Only two women seem aware of him.
One says *But this frees us. I'd be a fool* —
Say it with me, says the other. *For him to revive*
we must both say it. Say Be alive. —

But it was our own friends who got
him with a brave shot, a clever shot. —
Those are our equals: we scorn them
for being no more than ourselves.
Say it with me. Say Be alive. —

Elder sister, it is impossible. —
Life was once impossible. And flight. And speech.
It was impossible to visit the moon.
The impossible's our summoning dimension.
Say it with me. Say Be alive again.

The younger wavers. She won't leave
nor stop being furious. The sea's vast
catchment of light sends ashore a roughcast
that melts off every swimmer who can stand.
Glaring through slits, the storm moves inland.

The younger sister, wavering, shouts *Stay dead!*
She knows how impossibility
is the only door that opens.
She pities his fall, leg under one knee
but her power is his death, and can't be dignified.

GEOFF PAGE

It is difficult in these postmodern times to talk about 'intention' — and potentially immodest or foolish at any time. Who knows how far your work may fall short of its vainglorious 'aim'? I have heard poets constructing great spontaneous essays in the air about a bad poem directly in front of them.

Nevertheless, I will be old-fashioned enough to say that I do have aims when I'm working on a poem. Among them are the following:

1. To do justice to the original perception or impulse;

2. To satisfy an audience of one (myself) and then send the poem off in search of the rest of its audience (assisted by public readings where possible);

3. To construct 'a small machine made of words', as William Carlos Williams said, i.e. to ensure that every word contributes to the overall effect;

4. To make a small (sometimes infinitesimal) difference to the way people look at the issue addressed in the poem, i.e. most good poems have a degree of moral intent even if only subliminal and not fully comprehended by the poet.

Barthes and Derrida have assured us that the poem (or the language) writes itself. This is not very far from the idea of the muse and there's clearly some truth in it. A good poem is never written by intention alone. Why is it, though, that the muse is kinder to some poets than others? Could it be that, like the guy at the end of the Toyota assembly line, she's interested in quality control?

The Line

At 8 am one autumn Thursday
in a high-rise over Victoria Park
I watch the suburb weave itself,

a warp and woof of gums and elms.
I hear the scattered codes of dogs
with radios from secret kitchens

and note the buses on the cross streets
baulking at the Give Way signs.
The backs of birds are there below me,

magpies and the cockatoos
in easy swoops from pole to tree.
Across the softened city grid

some council will have half forgotten
I read the patterning of rooves,
the beaten tiles in need of mending

and here and there in certain driveways
a mixer with its hill of sand.
Early children start for school,

pick up a friend along the way
and further north a slate blue mist
is rising from the river.

The skyline of the city towers
strikes the eye but only briefly.
The suburb now spread out beneath me

is sewn into a single Thursday
quilted neatly piece by piece:
dogs and buses, kids and trees,

the birds which stitch it all together,
these tiles so mottled with the past.
A line arrives and is abandoned:

perfection of imperfect parts.

Thirteen Years

Thirteen years
the yachts lean round the point;
then ride up on their trailers

to float discreetly home.
Thirteen years
the clouds pass over

given back as in a mirror
or blow on up the lake in gusts
above its careful edges.

Thirteen years
the cars go by;
the joggers circulate at lunch

then vanish into public buildings.
The sun each day
dissolves into the mountains

and leaves its stain upon the water,
enamelling the evening reaches,
as twelve feet down

below the keels
and severed from the sound of traffic
a woman waits behind the wheel,

her key in the ignition.

The Stain

Like motor oil
through porous rock
it works its way

down from the top.
A journalist
in clever section

may show its slow descent ...
while from below
it seems to be

a watertable rising,
bearing its salt
towards the air,

a sour taste in
the mouth each day,
a lowered ceiling

for the spirit.
Our lives, so rich
in compromise,

are stooped between the two.
We work our
galleries of stone.

And see already
not far off
sump oil ride the ruined water.

Belanglo

The murderer
who works among us
is sometimes vague
but not unlike us

brings his lunchbox
in each day
does not complain
about the pay

gets no memo
from the wife
has talked of bushwalks
once or twice

takes a sickie
now and then
but no more so
than other men

wears a name that
some forget
and others haven't
noticed yet

pulls up in a
4 wheel drive
there by nine and
gone at five

shows no anxiety
for promotion
absorbed no doubt
with one emotion

the nursing of a
slow contempt
the pleas, the shrieks,
the arguments

the rucksacks, knife,
adrenalin,
the shallow graves
he sets them in

the dead now silent
in a smile
that doesn't yet
exist on file

the unseen, un-
accepting dead
who walk the fire trails
in his head

those moonlit gravels
white as bone …
the killer that
we've always known

DOROTHY PORTER

Poetry is my response to the delight — and dilemma — of awareness. I'm dismayed at how unpopular and marginalised poetry, at least in the English-speaking world, has become. My verse novels have been written chiefly to appease my own desire to meddle and pry, in true Doctor Jekyll fashion, with traditional notions of narrative and characterisation. I have also enjoyed throwing down the gauntlet and challenging the absurd idea that prose invented fiction. But I don't want my poetry to be too confined by the strictures of dramatic and narrative writing. Stevie Smith suggested, with her familiar deadly whimsy, every good poem has within it both Heaven and Hell. I dream of writing a poetry that takes the risk of the ineffable as well as the dare of the abyss.

PMT

The moon is out this morning.
Full,
        and the yellow
          of old dentures.
Nothing like a moon
        in a fastidious T'ang poem
it stares through
        the mist, the traffic, my windscreen,
like a mesmerising chilblain.

The radio is a box of Fantales;
        gossip, rubbish
          and caramel.
I chew on it
thinking about
        my long weekend
        my lover's delectable mouth.
But the moonlight
        splashes on my driving hands
          like freezing water
and I count my jerky heartbeats
        backwards.

Ebony Cats

(from the verse novel *Akhenaten*)

I preen and snigger
        when he talks to me
        when he looks at me
          like that.

His eyes are almonds.
I twitch

to pluck them out
and eat them
instead
 I play
 like one of my kids
with the ebony cats on the table
my fingers
 silly.

Touch me, he whispers
touch me, he insists
I froth at the mouth
swallow my tongue

where has the Good God gone?

helpless
I see the crops black
 up and down the river.

In A Good Light

A welcome swallow
swoops through
an open, high window
 of a research laboratory —

a mercurial sneak
 glimpse
 of colours
is its back blue?
is its throat red?
Falls
 like a four-leaf clover
comes up
 like matching fruit
 on a poker machine —

a monkey
in a restraining device
watches the bird
     and shivers
          with fear —

coffee rings on the long table
          gleam
     in a rod of sun;
a man
     fiddling with a bunsen burner
enjoys its sharp shadow
     in the shining morning,
its gas hiss
     of all systems go —

he strolls through
psychology's dark heart
     in a whistling, amiable
          white coat;
at home
     he has a dog,
          two cats
and dotes on them all —

he views pain
as a series of responses
     as complex, challenging
          as Rubik's cube;
an enigma
     of nerves and phantoms
that just needs
     a persistent twiddling
     in a clear light
this bright morning's
     light —

the swallow
     glides over his head
          like a charged particle
          in St Francis' bird halo,
the man's eyes soften
     at the acrobatic bird,

almost as terrific
as the silver twin-seater
                    he'd buy
if he won Lotto —

the flame of the burner
has a faint, but reeking
                    smell,
the monkey's heart
                    squirms;
he's been through this before.

Selected Verse

(from the chapter 'Verse and Jesus' in the verse novel
The Monkey's Mask)

A cup of coffee
a full pack of smokes

and my feet up

bribes
before I could face
Bill's *Selected Verse*

not even a double scotch
could get me through
this fucking poem

in twenty-three parts

finding God in a paddock
when Bill was full
of doubts and pimples

oh, mate,

we should swap
spiritual experiences

I'll never forget the day
I was full of the hots
and Diana's pink nipples.

Got Him

(from the chapter 'Verse and Jesus' in the verse novel
The Monkey's Mask)

I went through a bottle
of first class white
reading Mickey's poems

hundreds of them
in different inks
bad handwriting

I read them all

someone had ground her
in the dirt

her killer?

or were the poems
part of the fun?

tear me up
hurt me stuff

no
that's my scene
not Mickey's

she was young
in love
on the line

who isn't at nineteen?

Is Lou right?
was there more than one
beautiful man?

hard to imagine
taking the bastards
that seriously

but it was all there

the rush in the blood
the kick in the guts.

and something else

sweaty, nasty
like a missionary
with a prayer book
in one hand
and a damp erection
in the other.

Bill McDonald.

PETER PORTER

After fifty years of writing poetry I find it difficult to describe my intentions or even my hopes for development. It seems strangely consolatory that there should be poetry in the world, and that it is a fixed part of the landscape of the human mind. As one's career draws towards its conclusion, one is tempted to discern a shape to one's work, a sense that there has been a guiding strategy all along — 'rounded with a sleep', as it were. But the opposite is just as true: I find I approach each new poem with the same sense of setting out, of being a fledgling, which was the case when I began. I have written, I calculate, more than three thousand poems, of which mercifully I have suppressed at least half. Such unforgivable prodigality looks pretty meagre, however, when matched against Shelley's twice the output in less than thirty years. So, whatever the state of the overall poetic landscape, I raise my glass and toast myself, and look forward to the poems I have yet to write.

On First Looking Into Chapman's Hesiod

For 5p at a village fête I bought
Old Homer-Lucan who popped Keats's eyes,
Print smaller than the Book of Common Prayer
But Swinburne at the front, whose judgement is
Always immaculate. I'll never read a tenth
Of it in what life I have left to me
But I did look at *The Georgics*, as he calls
The Works and Days, and there I saw, not quite
The view from Darien but something strange
And balking — Australia, my own country
And its edgy managers — in the picture of
Euboeaen husbandry, terse family feuds
And the minds of gods tangential to the earth.

Like a Taree smallholder splitting logs
And philosophizing on his dangling billies,
The poet mixes hard agrarian instances
With sour sucks to his brother. Chapman, too,
That perpetual motion poetry machine,
Grinds up the classics like bone meal from
The abattoirs. And the same blunt patriotism,
A long-winded, emphatic, kelpie yapping
About our land, our time, our fate, our strange
And singular way of moons and showers, lakes
Filling oddly — yes, Australians are Boeotians,
Hard as headlands, and, to be fair, with days
As robust as the Scythian wind on stone.

To teach your grandmother to suck eggs
Is a textbook possibility in New South Wales
Or outside Ascra. And such a genealogy too!
The Age of Iron is here, but oh the memories
Of Gold — pioneers preaching to the stringybarks,
Boring the land to death with verses and with
Mental Homes. 'Care-flying ease' and 'Gift-
Devouring kings' become the Sonata of the Shotgun
And Europe's Entropy; for 'the axle-tree, the quern,
The hard, fate-fostered man' you choose among
The hand castrator, kerosene in honey tins
And mystic cattlemen: the Land of City States
Greets Australia in a farmer's gods.

Hesiod's father, caught in a miserable village,
Not helped by magic names like Helicon,
Sailed to improve his fortunes, and so did
All our fathers — in turn, their descendants
Lacked initiative, other than the doctors' daughters
Who tripped to England. Rough-nosed Hesiod
Was sure of his property to a slip-rail —
Had there been grants, he'd have farmed all
Summer and spent winter in Corinth
At the Creative Writing Class. Chapman, too,
Would vie with Steiner for the Pentecostal
Silver Tongue. Some of us feel at home nowhere,
Others in one generation fuse with the land.

I salute him then, the blunt old Greek whose way
Of life was as cunning as organic. His poet
Followers still make me feel déraciné
Within myself. One day they're on the campus,
The next in wide hats at a branding or
Sheep drenching, not actually performing
But looking the part and getting instances
For odes that bruise the blood. And history,
So interior a science it almost seems
Like true religion — who would have thought
Australia was the point of all that craft
Of politics in Europe? The apogee, it seems,
Is where your audience and its aspirations are.

'The colt and mule, and horn-retorted steer' —
A good iambic line to paraphrase.
Long storms have blanched the million bones
Of the Aegean, and as many hurricanes
Will abrade the headstones of my native land:
Sparrows acclimatize but I still seek
The permanently upright city where
Speech is nature and plants conceive in pots,
Where one escapes from what one is and who
One was, where home is just a postmark
And country wisdom clings to calendars,
The opposite of a sunburned truth-teller's
World, haunted by precepts and the Pleiades.

The Easiest Room In Hell

At the top of the stairs is a room
one may speak of only in parables.

It is the childhood attic,
the place to go when love has worn away,
the origin of the smell of self.

We came here on a clandestine visit
and in the full fire of indifference.

We sorted out books and let the children
sleep here away from creatures.

From its windows, ruled by willows,
the flatlands of childhood stretched
to the watermeadows.

It was the site of a massacre,
of the running down of the body
to less even than the soul,
the tribe's revenge on everything.

It was the heart of England
where the ballerinas were on points
and locums laughed through every evening.

Once it held all the games,
Inconsequences, Misalliance, Frustration,
even *Mendacity, Adultery* and *Manic Depression.*

But that was just its alibi,
all along it was home,
a home away from home.

Having such a sanctuary
we who parted here
will be reunited here.

You asked in an uncharacteristic note,
'Dwell I but in the suburbs
of your good pleasure?'

I replied, 'To us has been allowed
the easiest room in hell'.

Once it belonged to you,
now it is only mine.

Landscape With Orpheus

'Man lebt nur einmal, dies sei dir genug'.

It was as if the film had stuck, he was always
Back at the point where he moved up the latch
And stood facing down the street, aware of
The cicadas turning themselves on in both tall
And dumpy trees: what he saw was limited
But included lakes of dirt-in-asphalt
Before his feet, the unfortunate slug about
To cross the pavement with no more instinctive
Knowledge of its danger than he had of the sun
Perhaps on his neck, and of course always
The Dutchman's Pipe flowers he never failed
To notice, their purple mouthpieces like Disney
Saxophones, edible, sexual and howling for the dead.

It would take a lifetime to make it to the ferry,
A sunstroke's distance amid pavilioned leaves
And so desirable an ending. Well, there was a life
To spend and this was time, the softest element,
Like sap from poinsettia leaves, the milky pus
Of dreams — Eyes stood on tiptoes in those hedges,
So perhaps he should begin. It was late and it was early
In his sorrow and he had the world's tunes to play
And a landscape of peace and obsession there —
To see it all stretched out and hardly a step taken,
Such was the gift of time, walking down to the ferry

With love to come and snake-bite and the bitches flying
As calm as tapestry, in light-soaked Poussin shades.

Praise of his bloodstream flowed on then in sounds.
That this untrained imagination out of mercantile
Forebears should be Emperor of Cadences didn't surprise,
Don't we all know we are immaculate in our dress
Of self, and the twenty billion succinct souls
Hanging on God are just light in the distance
By which pilgrim feet find tracks to follow,
And that this fold of fact would undo and show
A hidden nothing if we blinked? The place of the ordinary
Is on the throne: save afternoons for judgement
And every morning for our table music. Could he have
Passed the big house with the haunted windows
And nipple-pointed fence, he had hardly moved?

But the stickiness underfoot was disquieting,
Perhaps the land was Avernus, with those
Bamboo raggednesses above the fence and the pale smell
Of warm tar on the air. Through fur of sugar-grass
He saw the river and all remote existence
Sculling across the darkened tide. What blew in his face
Were words, those he would speak in love and those
Which fattened on betrayal. The words for death
Were still unknown and yet he knew they sought him
On the street. A wind of big mothers mixing drinks
Caught him suddenly with laughter. What if he got
To the wharf, what if the ferry with a Lady's Name
Were there? He sang, in case, 'Goodnight, deceiving world!'

The cicadas stopped. Silence grew into a theatre
With everybody watching. According to the small print,
When love has failed to come you choose your end
By divination. Child or old man, now is the hour
And memory's prevarication cannot last.
With final breath whisper us your Eins, Zwei, Drei.
The sun in intervention breaks the sky,
The camera is rewound and there is the old latch,
The gate, the pepperina tree, the ferry rounding
Onions Point. The future must be crowded into now,
Paradise and hell on deck. Viewed through the telescope,
The Town Hall clock shows Orpheus looking back.

Timing The Gerberas

Everything in the garden's lovely
say the introduced sub-species
galloping up their galvanising trellises,
buttering the sun with raucous saffron
so even beige is capable of glowing —
the incinerator, the compost-heap, the couch-grass clippings
insist that all's right with the world,
bougainvillea storming past the privet,
tireless the gardener as he kills and saves.

The natives are becoming restless
is the lost report of desert winds,
the tramontana's silica
brings leaves down from some last bushfire
and rebirth knocks at roots as dry as ticks —
absolute Eden is a legend
when a snake may be a rainbow
or a river-course; gestalt gives
its blessing to the millenarians.

The world is all before us, where to choose,
declare those universalists who've never heard
of any home but where they are, their sap
a six-lane highway no adventurer has reached
and expatriation just a change of clothes —
garish gerberas, sub-Franciscan solipsists,
glorify the present, charge the sun
to do its duty, shining, shining on,
the genius of the place rouged in their eye.

PETER ROSE

Every poem is a kind of essay in quandariness (to use Frank O'Hara's fine coinage), but the five published in this anthology seem to point to a couple of directions in my recent work. 'Late Division' is a fairly straightforward, if eclectic, narrative poem, commencing, as is often the case with my poetry, with some family lore then veering off in all sorts of oxymoronic directions. On the other hand, the genesis of poems like 'In Your Story' or 'Georgian Dream' is so weird, so capricious, if you like, I marvel all over again at the defiant otherness of poetry. I would find it difficult, for instance, to unravel 'Greening', except to say that, deplorably or not, it's not about environmentalism.

Perfect Pitch

Perhaps there are no windows
in that perfect space,
only the towers of consolation
and a rational landscape —
one asp, sole cypress,
the vacant madonna.
We have stared so long
the insights avert their faces,
unnerved by such needfulness.
Less agile than fantasy, we
surrender to a documentary past
no longer gratifying —
squeamish, derisory.
Always qualifying, always
going back. It is the tendency
our enemies like least.
That girl is massacring his hair
and he is deeply stirred.
Later, afternoon releasing him,
he will move into himself,
the unattended room, no longer
craving water, solace, air,
impatient of such perquisites.

Georgian Dream

Moments before dawn,
the black outline of a terrace
forms like Manet's gallows.
Preternaturally awake,
the elongated self is led away
protesting not his own
or anyone else's innocence
but his amatoriness,
that it was his sister not his drawn self
who betrayed the capital.
When the instrument of hands
removes his cowl,
accuses him of promiscuity,
he regrets only the manner of his syntax.
This will chivvy the choice, the grand,
along the abject boulevard.

Greening

Let's not watch the main event,
let's watch the people.
There we shall be beautifully private,
each lake with its own suicide,
those grand disclosures
aching on a beach.
Your beauty is the last quotation,
an available dark.
In the forest, single lights flicker,
day rapturously evokes night.
Soon we shall descend
into the public acre,
a rhapsodist will forfeit
his throne by the view.
So let's postpone matter for a while:
the ritual caper, an auspicious turn.

Late Division

I am in East Melbourne again,
born next door at the cocktail hour,
twelve hours' nemesis then
a leaky lung. All of us were born
in some vicinity — two names
suffice for this struggle. When
they flung those Catholic bells
for my brother our mother
thought she was in heaven.
Merely a king had died.
Long we keep on going back:
infant, chorister, lover,
now the duteous friend.
But it feels late tonight,
too chill for martinis' shock
and brio. Hunched in scarves
we tack through terraced streets,
almost afraid of this wind,
meet the poet who will read to us,
complaining of laryngitis.
Beyond the park, the bells of state
summon late representatives
and the brilliant Princess tolls
for smokers in cummerbunds.
Bolting like truants,
cashmered staffers quit Parliament
via the royal entrance,
though the bells go on ringing.
It's late, very late now
in the galvanic Writers' Centre
where four of us have gathered —
more casks than aesthetes.
Upstairs has been rented out
for a Self-esteem Workshop.
During breaks in the urban arias
we hear them moving about
like confident roof-rats.
They leave before us, looking bullish.

In Your Story

after Edward Albee

This obliquity is almost shining,
those eyes of a different colour.
In your story we are all triptychs,
dynasties of pearly selves,
needing so many acts to intermit
a flawed heart, the loping silence.
Cloudage, suspended or real,
ushers rancour, vindication.
Across orchestras, promenades,
immortals step onto a terrace,
admire the infinite, humanized greenery.
What curious lives they must lead
in their tumid, adulterous valleys;
spontaneity the gods, endamaged, lack.
New perspectives, severely raked,
take our lines away, dispossessed.
In a park, day perpetrates its farce,
merchants, selling palmery,
glide backwards in their noble tans.
The children are gathering autumn.
They do not understand yet —
the falconer ignores their plight.
Your character would identify
with this sorrow, this realized joy.
The soliloquy at the end baffles
old perplexities; we ease them
with our random gait. Like Spartans
of some consummate struggle, martyrs
brandish china and speakers, veer
northward, skyward, rearward, anyways.

PETER ROSE

Terminus

The whorl inside my head buzzes,
this cog which no one can replicate.
Somewhere you lie dying,
given till midnight.
You fell down on a tram,
blacked out between terminals,
fit, bright, twenty-one.
Puccini gave Manon an aria
but it hardly seems to matter much.
No doubt they shrank
from your devastating touch,
ricking their necks
in an effort not to look,
just as I, unable to fathom
this ruin, this mystery,
this topical egg,
pause for a moment
before going on with
my re-read novel, my *TLS*.

GIG RYAN

GIG RYAN

He Extrapolates

1

It's not that I bent to her will,
or changed in any elemental way, but to keep the peace,
to keep her, I postponed opinion, let it hover in my head
and not protrude into our clinch. For her
everything was definite. I tend to be less set —
flowers and knives chatter in me. She couldn't hear
above the din of definition how I was slipping off.
Evidence and application were her fields,
I liked the scrawls they made
Motivation slept, books draped
then I had depressed and it was grey
the ashtray CDs hanged like cards

2

Time ticks through the hot and cold water flats
I love the Rwandan CD I don't espouse
The pygmy tribe they found was great
I concentrate to remember those I'm with
If I could, I would sing of love
Aspiring, unsuccessfully, to wealth
I stay home and hear her saga mope and taiwan blinds ladder sleep

Disinformation

1

The fireworks of peace and celebration go up in the harbour
above the warships. Sailors strut through town
adored to skint women who, for a job, will cheer their garish flag
One's trippy and bursts into the flat
jawing the air with a knife.
He was disinformed. The pictures, the hype
that rev a plane across the Gulf of Sidra
mill in his baseball head until Intelligence chucks him

2

Our clown Prime Minister jostles on the steps,
unable to dissemble,
unable to not be loved by Indonesia, France, Chile, China
He troths the Bases, not alienated anymore
He clucks his timely personality
The sin of doubt assails the booths
He holds his broken minister in a camera grip
and weeps a tub
'Your women are beautiful,' says the Yank
in relay with his Navy darkening the harbour

Love's Pillage

The false drugged light in your face
I mean, mate, it was sick city
when you bungled towards me
His eyes like golfballs
a briny convocation
I collapse in your gagged kiss
stuck on weeks
I clock on like a silencer

The night carves out its attack
He takes off his mask of care
the dumb sterile arms you build
to be safe, gradually eliminating all
that affects you
the deathless glass pyramid you slide in like a will

This is the last straw, he shows himself wet
He patches things up
He returns to death
holding it in his long arms like a job
He goes under
whereas I don't, except with mourning

They get hospitalized
not you, bravely pandering to a concept
Sorrow's old classic taste
washes out my mouth
The rain spiders lurch in the window's open black strip
I tame my neck with drugs
Phoney extroversion brought him home
but now coming down, like a saint
his sharp Lucretian body jerks up the stairs
Love's pillage

Import

Loneliness chucks out before me like a rug
its bleak subtext of despair
I walk a thousand times
your nowhere streets
Lost, like them
bearing from a distance the lies that got you hopeful
Your soul, acting like the last straw
A humanoid darkness hedges me
this wearing cycle where I die and surface
Go back to the country, Secretive
Here, I try my head inside the wall

It builds back up,
away from love's odour and the numb girlfriend
cooling outside
You get concerned, suddenly, for your dying friends
and get fit
I'm looking through you, weak with boredom
It was months, baby,
her slow suburbs dwell and hold it like a toast
For me, it was brash
Since then I've been circling
and offer you the world

I extinguish it, that stuff
I'd converted into hard currency, you know,
correct because lasting
It ended up being foreign, not legit.,
a sort of warping in the air
Desire dresses bravely up
I crush the lighted door
The kid looks after me
We shelter beside the pool of voyeurism
Marriages go past, austere hypocrite

Pure and Applied

1

The channel caves in his hand like a weak cushion
as news read the screen
and curved along its poverty, a reflecting and equivalent desert
occupies geometry
which devalues each tincture my chatelaine
which people vacancy
like today's harping and the litmus of his hair

2

Politicians nod like priests
You slip in the crowded chair like 3 million others
TV shows you
The rest is dreck, a slump
You surrender to his embalming pill
his glorious forgotten blockout kiss and nest
The walls' diagrams arrowing to a former heaven peter in the mind
Monotonous branches scratch the ditchy air
I had to look at 800 dollars
but death precedes me entering like worthlessness

3 (the good weekend)

Ten pages on a headache A world satisfied by charisma
The corner shop's dim globes the newspaper's parting atoms
but death can be 'egotistical, manipulative', his claim and corona
Her burying mother acridly grinds into the present
An article probes the shops, the ultras
in the sad dark regions and recesses of his relation

The sheets wind milky green
and then a big blue sky's supposed to incize
putting you in the right counsel
I watch his weakness strive and shut
as theory wades, but on practice it's a klutz

I protect him from ardour
Here, in this propensity, this rust
My paraphernalia crash in a junction of boredom

4

Automatically he'd be a lump
The light's suicide split craving beneath the wax door
Piano tinkles over the woolknit-lounge ad, his thoughts
that mirror a wreath of gloss abrupt pages
perspex and disheartened and foam
dead desire
and he uncrumples from the black lacquer

5 (sum)

'It bores me severely
Everything you say is thrashed into a refrained verdict
numbfully secure at its post
The car's underwater the doorkey starts
and recedes like a gun, excellently
and never loved. Obstruct, by all means, any silent rack or behest
Anyway, it was major which you blasted, a real user

He was glamourized, delta'd, totally miami'd
like a shoot-out, you know, head above water
His blue hair shining like rockets
Dance-a-rama I'll say, you should've seen the gronks
they turned away in squadrons, rapturously
to the new spasmic floor. I could've killed
but I dropped stuff instead
and was, subsequently, messed for any social, being severely zomboid
Last night: what a crack'

TRACY RYAN

Generally I would prefer the work to speak for itself. Comments on possible directions are quickly dated: I find out as I go along. Current material is heavily affected by cultural dislocation, but that will not yet be evident in the poems selected here. What is consistent is an interest in, and an immersion in, processes of language, especially in terms of the effects of foreign-language learning, and lately being involved (both ways) in translation. These things are not necessarily content but context. Writing neither from England nor from Australia but returning 'from afar, from always: from "without", from the heath where witches are kept alive ...' (Cixous, *The Laugh of the Medusa*).

Hair

The length
of my body is an odd
nudity, what is it
doing there, how
did the hair
get pared down
to just
these patches
we cultivate
like fetishes
meant to excite
when we want
to play animal
or we control
to stress and make
the difference
between sexes
as if otherwise
we couldn't find
ourselves.
I can't force
what once was
to grow now
in a strange season
I'm caught between
the dream of befores
that paralyses
and the need
of my own nakedness
which is there,
which is there.

Cycle

I am pressing these tiny tacks out
& into my body
securing freedom

sending the womb
messages like sweets
my mother told me never
to take from strangers

I am shelling the days neatly
as peas that will never reach
the table, I am

exercising control, choosing
carefully
my mistakes.

Sand

Where little bits of us got lost forever —
mystery never resolved, how it could wholly
swallow a marble or matchbox car.
We'd bore small tunnels that always collapsed
though shored hard, arms furred with crystals
as we pulled out. We'd heard of cave-ins that
filled bodily holes with golden amalgam,
dry drowning. So solid, yet shifting
like those grains in the wheat bin that
also terrified, seed reclaiming flesh
for clay. And the way it could
sting you to blindness if pitched
even in innocence, warm antipodean
version of the snowball, covering all.

Trompe l'oeil

Look how the table's becoming
a table again,
as coach turns to pumpkin
only slower.

The marquetry's starting
to separate, making
rips in the fabric
of deception

just as my face takes rifts
under the same old daily
make-up, flesh begging
to differ.

It's as if the picture
were failing
through lack of someone's
faith

but who is it asking?
Who was that letter meant for
& what were the downturned cards
about to tell?

Our fingers want
to pick them up
but slip on glaze
rebarbative as mirrors,
itch over coins, quill, signet
& sealing wax.

Some kind of hoax
Was it a joke only contemporaries
were meant to get,

an innocent talking point,
favourite set-piece?

Or did Boilly suspect we'd stand here
two centuries later
by his elaborate *memento mori*
still marvelling at his virtual skill,

the willing eye
a hopeless romantic that
can only be cheated?

Potatoes

Why eyes when these are fingers,
wriggling out, obscene,
revealed in the low closet
by my child, seeking treasures.
Uprooted from any element,
they roll and wobble — too small
or odd for any meal,
passed over yet not tossed out,
despite reminders,
broodily shooting purple feelers, flesh
sagged as the back of my father's hands
digging and pressing.
Later I watched him
tugging the stems gone dry
a whole plant spent for its
coveted roots, this nest of eggs
plundered by little accomplices.
Now I am looking for good ones
to feed us, scrubbing & gouging
till half the substance is gone.

Penguin Island

By pure chance catching
the last boat of the last
day of the season

building on a connection others think
tenuous as this vanishing
sandbank where the sign warns
LIVES HAVE BEEN LOST

we cross and head for the summit
like making Stations
at each stop meditating

not on suffering but
on regeneration —

gulls' eggs fallen
from a high nest yet
intact, perfect
in abandonment,

on movement through
recuperating dunes and around
brooding penguins only the subtle ear
can sense

touching and leaving things as
we know we must
each other — as found.

PHILIP SALOM

I am taken by poetry that wears (and sometimes wears out with great panache) all that poetry has been in the past and anything that it can try new. I like it lively and inventive but with feel. Sounds impure, and it is. This means taking on poetry as segue. I desire this feeling of frisson, knowing its diversity may produce a fractured sonnet, a post-modern lyric: spare words and 'accessibility' through a poet's 'voice', images across time and place/s, styles and references. Poetry also as a dig at itself, a bone buried in the symbolic garden, a deconstruction of what had been ... I admired Dennis Potter's *The Singing Detective* for its acerbic humour and its ironic toughening of those nostalgic songs, for the big attractive tropes and shifts of detective fiction ... deeply poetic ... And I want poetry to create a strange music and even a sense of ontological investigation, words performing much more than mimesis, but emphasising the place where poetry and the world are merged: where the making both finds and empties the world in the poem.

But never empties it too much: I feel words must 'give' and I judge poems harshly when they don't give enough ... I want to feel the stuff kick me, I want passion and emotion but always intelligence, imagination but with grounding. I do not want Romantic gestures. I want to write poems and find other people's poems where these things make me sit back, arrested by the language and the knowing/constructing something I had not.

The Stone Operas

1

This is the kind of mood when all the rational will not do
and dam walls are heavier than dreams, the walls of Khajaru
out-love us, the greatest statues worry us, they take up more
than was given, as if they know

where Paul's severed
head struck the ground
and bounced, there are
now three churches

the impossibility of fully
describing a document
or the intent of a request
without ambiguity or
needing to answer yet
another question

what is best and worst of us and ignore it.

In dreams I've heard them start: the first stone
like the whinneying of a mare, a chorus from Aeschylus
cramming every station of the Orient Express.

The old world is heavy... with witches from Macbeth, or Tasmania's blacks in
nets of grieving, the deaths of children from starvation, leg-irons
gangrenous in the wind, agonies of births, love-cries from anywhere,

polyphonic opera

20 million refugees   the baby falls in

at sea like travelling   the pond higher in
                           moonlight
as a power-boat

but whose nation is   plop of the old frog

not Christ upon the

of the dead. The world's too small/too big:
the world hatched and won't take in
islands, their one compass shaking
approaches, and like them runs no flag,
piracy and rape, Oh he is a pirate king
water. It's not the post-modern condition

any more than abacus rattle like a reassuring
sum, or computers mutter on each disk
their tiny runes. Theory won't annul.

The ruthless are immortal, they will
file their nails and do paperwork of heaven,
and distrust passion. Someone always,
someone always wants to do the killing.
Except we see and hear it like a programme.

Oh Dear, what can the matter be?
Oh Dear, what can the matter be?
Oh Dear, what can the matter be?
Johnny's so long at the.....

Israeli troops shot dead three
Palestinian policemen. It sounded
as if she said: How do you repair
them? How do you repair us
now they've gone?

2

The world

is the worst the best the only opera and we are drafted

to the chorus, always the locked-up repetition of the words

country by country, the hopeless crush against the wire,

or from our own mouths like a spiel for a useless product,

a cry for the self, when there is all this, heavy

as stones in the spine

like a dumb waiter.

There is no one place

these all started

but they end loaded

on tectonic arks to

slide around

on grinding engines.

The driver of the drilling rig was then given instructions to go straight into tribal land, where the crew would join him and begin

All systems, by training and indoctrination, may enslave their followers and even their leaders. The obsessive is captive to the obsession. In ordinary systems ignorance makes people assume nobody is a slave. Look around and tell me who is not a slave...
Even by open-ness: tell them to question and you have captured their questioning. Accept their criticism with much nodding and intelligent backing down then do as you wanted, they will lose their power to intervene, you will have captured their intervention.

They fall from bomb-bays, through unseen flares

of television wavering at night like the karma of our crazed

sensations, like the Aurora Borealis flames, like white-ocean loss

of trees falling in bitter settings. They are the ground-bass

and bottom registers of our minds, the truth tripping on the furniture

at Newstime.

beautiful, the

through valleys

sum of the sum

When she walked past the flower-seller
the perfume distracted her, the armfulls
of purple, yellow, red, but she caught
her heel in the cracked pavement pain
rushed in her like a whiplash

The weather is too

wind is almost sexual

and catchments, the

of everything is quite

impossible. And so much that's said is just denial put like promises

like Buddha's final pain or righteousness, as if death is circular,

and the endless store of the world's free-will turns like a grindstone.

3

I watch fireworks at night under their fiery-cold elation. The suffering

that's casually forgotten, the dreams that fall on other cultures.

Impossibly, I estimate the weight of colours, textures of flame.

Frankenstein is
tottering away
Mary Shelley's
fear or hurt at
what she grew
from as the
birth her mother
died from, the
child she later
lost, the poets
who took her on
without looking
the monster she
saw at the heart
of all creation

There is always the nearness of answers. Something seduces.

Something is weightless in us. The day, the cities, the nations

are never innocent, something is always *wrong*... So many

would-be saints, or magnates wanting epics, stare at stone,

imagining they'll dash their rhetoric against it, and find God

or oil, or economic theory, cliffs of cities rising like revelations

full of awful operas. The stones weigh on us like poverty.

But we resist them, we give them back their heads and hearts,

ineffable characters. We worry for survival. We love ruins.

PHILIP SALOM

Woken In Melaka

All night the wind past the upper storeys
howls like a jet falling.
                          Woken, unnerved,
wanting sleep, wanting not to think, but
it's not thinking, this howl's far older.
Our window's flush as vertigo with the light
glaring from the nerves of streets below
where people drive all night like jolts
of light against the tower. This hotel,
the Ramadan Renaissance, silver and vast
above the modest buildings. And the wind
which screams like a jet falling. I stare
down, woken, where Allah never sleeps:
his Renaissance returning all night past
the upper storeys — I see Iran, the old
Iran that gave us the Future. But now its
ayatollahs howl to take it back, honing
the past to an edge against the upper
storeys.
        I hear it in Old Melaka, but
the howl's far older than Allah and all
our jets. It's the earth's primal screaming.
I stare down from the window at the glare.
All reassurance falls away.

Voyage And Recall

Fat and twenty-one, he left the cabin
chanting its number like a mantra,
returning hours later, panic in his eyes.
Lost at sea while still on board.
The numbers tumbled back to zero. Om.

Every day. His memory like a shredder
but when I sang in the shower it gave
Ta-ra-ra-boom-de-ay back to him
so we set the empty number to a song.
Passengers would hear him singing
down the long air of the passages.

I listened to the old man who said
the same boy's hands were perfect for piano.
But how would he keep concertos in?
We thought of John Ogdon, pudgy-fingered,
brilliant, remembering the depths too well,
until it was the depths he tumbled in
regardless of the numbers and the notes.

Each night a fine spray fell upon the old
man's face from the porthole above his bunk,
like something holy. His words were gentle
as his convalescence after heart-attack,
calm as the moonlight on the upper decks
he never saw; his throat was gaunt and veined
as his body on the table must have been
with tubes and the sequences of survival.

Three of us, for a week, unalike, the same.
And I, carried with them, somehow *trying*
to get lost, tumbling through the sequences
of distance: escaping with my art and youth
in order to be found. The classic scene!
Each of us glad the world was somewhere else.
The man-boy's eyes and the old man's throat
later I would paint. And lose the painting.

Time is air now and we fly through it.
I return to this ship like a poem I must live,
having ended up a poet, and poetry being
more the Fairstar than Singapore Airlines,
deeply and for days at a time:
walking each night the decks under moonlight,
trays crashing from the steward's hands in the Bight,
Yossarian prevaricating with the mad
in the deepest cinema I've ever sat in.

Singing the numbers like a mantra,
like the shock and song of imagery falling
upon the heart, wild-eyed or calm,
the spray coming down less like annunciation
than the deep handshake of words.
Opening at last the cabin door.

ANDREW SANT

I'm open to developments across a broad front, but there's an exploratory element in my poetry which preoccupies me. This seems given to make matters transparent that are elusive or just a hunch, prior to a poem being written. Its genesis is likely to be triggered by initial observation; less frequently by print. The way a poem proceeds, the connections it makes, relies as much on instinct as intellect. This might also be true for poems with a social dimension, though the material they draw on has a prior hold on the outcome. Form is always a challenge, and therein lies a way of telegraphing fresh utterance. Ultimately, the poems I pursue generate connections (via imagery, sound ...), aim to be fully wired up.

Wren

A wren appears on the branch like an asterisk —

I refer back through
memory to a time of more constant
immersion of self in details —
once this would have been complete experience,
the wren offering itself
for my abandonment in detail,
landing on the fuchsia,
shaking the million purple bells
of my delight.
                    The wren flies off.
I'm left with a footnote of detail
towards an imminent theme.

Origin of the Species

My daughter has captured
wild animals upon sheets
of butchers' paper —

giraffes, apes, possums,
snakes, camels, hippos,
while all afternoon the wind

has shrieked outside like a hyena,
tearing off leaves, kicking
dustbins along the street.

Now her mind is a zoo
that lands an ark
of animals at will;

and they're also free
in the breakfast cereal,
each grinning like a Cheshire cat.

The wind exhausted,
we go outside and discover
a fledgling sparrow on the path.

With 'scientific interest'
I see its tiny bellows-
like lungs won't pump

much longer although
for millions of years this effort
has been relayed.

It will not fly
I tell her; she says it will
and later imagines this

on paper. I bury it where
neither tooth and claw nor theory
will interrupt this perfect flight.

Mussolini's Umbrella

For now the umbrella
will be banned from the house
as a traitor to rugged
complexions. *Ombrello* —
little shadow; too cute,
mused Il Duce, amid
this century's downpour
of bullets. It rises
abruptly as the national debt
and parades street to street
as a weakness. Let there be
hailstorms, heat, thunder
like jackboots striding
terrible skies; let
them bravely flush out
from cupboard or carboot
this conspicuous wretch
which given speech and
a dig in the ribs might confess
his dandy cheek is the
similitude of a rose
or a peach. Exile
this pansy to wasteland
or the muteness of movies;
seek it if it's stalled
in a cavernous hallway
like a tropical bat —
for it is the downfall
of national weather
and shelters a shadow
where there should be a lout.

Taking My Daughter To The Cave

Outside it's the New World; clean air,
damp ferns; a hole surprised by loggers
toppling the future one afternoon,
its thunder, ground shudder, ours for keeps.

The blackness theirs. It takes a guide,
flick of a switch, to scare with light
the million-years-old cave monster, fear,
and hear it trickle like a stream

through rock fissured, sure enough,
by continental drift, to where
no proto life-form shows the way.
Here might big questions arise again.

Should it seem more strange to hazard
answers underground than in the car
or leaf-strewn street where progress
derides what's out-of-date? My sweet,

my kid, my china plate, there might
have sprung a revolution in fast-food
or linguistics while, amid cave
spiders and beetles, we're diverted

by a stalagmite whose lit growth,
in a century, you'll shame within
a week. We hear its name. Well,
that's affectionate, tamed as stars.

Or echoes. Voices. Curiosity.
So lead us, comrade, past formations,
'The Wedding Cake', 'Tower of Pisa',
or whatever tricks the light proposes.

ANDREW SANT

Cover-up

It occurred to me that since our house was built in the 1860s
it must be made of convict bricks; now, scouring a wall, it occurs to me again
that behind plaster and paint there are convict bricks,
some with a sweaty thumbprint signature, convict colophons,
baked into orange clay and as permanent as those other inscriptions,
the welts of the lash that encouraged these walls piecemeal out of the ground;
and it occurs to me that each brick forms part of an unwritten history blasted
by a hell-fire that could bake a million bricks: a few thousand here
with solid life-everlasting behind plaster and paint.
I could expose and study them, they are those convicts' only gravestones
as befits the anonymity of those wearers of dun-coloured uniforms
but I'll keep them sealed off, not only for practical purposes
but also from better society. I think of the brogue of the Irish
and the witty cockney tale-spinners exiled in Tasmania
behind the hugely substantial indifference of distance;
and I am walled in, a keen listener amongst the dumb bricks, with windows
wide-open to admit the fresh breeze, the sail-raising westerlies.

Reading For Pleasure

I visit you and you tell me
of the books that you've devoured
in recent weeks, nervously
going for a cigarette, coffee, something
to hold, in need of reassurance.
The walls are lined
with books, and also stacked
like children's blocks: it's
a serious game you play.
This, I suppose, is companionship
since, now your wife's gone,
you live alone — though
not by choice; a restrained way

286

of living in a world on your own terms.
Though it does not make you happy.
What you digest is analytical —
politics, sociology, semiotics,
which leaves you well disposed
to criticise the revelations
of the daily press, and others.
Your talk is endless
confession, getting it
off your chest in the hope,
perhaps, of retrieving a convert
from the mess. I know it must
be serious being a priest.
Devotion maybe, but I too
have read and could announce
my findings — all this retention
a result of an infant anal complex.
My friend, you're stuffed with facts!
If you've read the jargon
of those secular priests
we don't discuss it, psychologism
is a bind I guess.
But then, that brimming lilac
you hadn't noticed at your door
is also worldly, a sensual
fact, uncluttered, buoyant, in the evening air.
Read into it, perhaps,
this disclosure: you must continue
to let go, before you start to savour …

287

ANDREW TAYLOR

When I wrote the long sequence, 'Sandstone', I was consciously trying to put together the two ends of my life so far, in the sense that I grew up beside the coast in Western Victoria, and now found myself living beside another coast, this time in Western Australia. Although vastly different, these two coastlines have been very important to me, and my move to Western Australia gave me the opportunity to view my childhood and adolescence from the perspective of a new experience of the coast on the other side of the country.

Coastlines are a major part of Australian life. But for me they also represent something that all my poetry has been involved in — the dividing line between what can be conceptualised and what cannot, between what can be said, and what evades language. It seems to me that language can say a great deal, and our everyday use of it is based on the assumption that it can say almost everything.

But poetry for me is a venture towards what cannot be said, towards what remains stubbornly and tantalizingly silent. This is why poets have to resort to such tricks as rhyme, rhythm, metaphor, ellipsis, breaks and silences. These are not decorations or embellishments, but strategies to lure the unsayable closer to speech. Poetry should have the ambition to chart the outline, the coastline, of what can and cannot be said, and this is what I hope mine will continue to do.

from Sandstone

10

I never believed in freak waves. I still don't.
Families swept from rock ledges, children
scooped from placid pools, fishermen tempting
one last cast into a rising surf — I'd sympathise
with their distraught relatives but not with them.

Anyone who has stood a day or two
even ankle deep in the sluice of open ocean
on mussel-covered rocks as the tide
drifts up and down, it seems, without purpose
or malice, should know better than that.

Those little waves like pups nibbling my ankles
are the real freaks. The biggish ones that nudge
at my knees are more honest. And when I see
the horizon crinkle and darken I run because
the sea is coming to itself, I know, and to me.

11

How do I keep a grip
on this continent, my life
clinging to its edges, cliffs
beaches? As days
fray into nights, and weeks
stretch empty, how do I

hold onto *here*, when you
are as usual elsewhere
and desire like a sunflower
plots your bright transit
over and out of reach?

By the sand between your toes
wind answers, by rain
in your face, by scars
in your memory, by force.

18

Such a conglomerate
of silica and little shells.
Little deaths. This sandstone
shelter from the wind, our puny
destinies heaping against
the granite of childbirth, death, against
a tectonic end to the sea's
ceaseless motion. Streets start here
and politics and negotiation. Here
the future begins
and the past lives, in talk. Sand
is as much of itself as the sea
permits, against granite law
to transact, poised, never still,
multiple, shifty, divisible.

19

At Warrnambool as you look
south at the Southern Ocean
that's the world's end. Past
that horizon and you've had it. If

the world is indeed flat, it's
here, near the old High School
where every now and then the island
would float inshore for an hour or two

then dissolve in a vapour
of astonishment. Beyond that
occasional visit the world ends.
My fishermen schoolmates know that.

Beyond the shark fisheries, beyond
the winds' invisible hatchery
our world stops. That's where we fall off.

20

'This is a fishing town, right?
Get one thing straight!
Fish come out of the sea.
Fish, I said. Maybe

a man too, if he's foolish enough
to stand too close to the edge
of something bigger than he
imagined, might slip

and if he's lucky we'll catch him.
Or maybe not. This
is the seventies now
not the roaring forties'.

His half million dollar boat
floats a little still in the future
next to me at school, in 1958.

21

Naked as sin
that's what they thought
and what we read
in their evasive eyes

as we asked them what
were they digging for
on an empty beach?
Naked as dolphins

obviously we'd been
while their Toyota
for at least eight k
busy with shovels

had scarred a line
where the sea withdrew
and we began.

30

Sand, I don't understand it.
I hold it in my hand and my grasp
appears in X-ray as the beach
reaches from my fingers' hooks
a shadow relief that might have been
a hand against the crawl and
tease of tide. That's not
my grip, my muscle, my long
burnt shoulders' complicity
and protest at decay. Sand
is miniscule bone, it hugs
flesh, toes, shins. I don't understand
how we can turn into sand, who
love it as beaches, houses, who
love more than our own dismay.

31

A continent crumbles and stops
and drops here to a bed of white sand
beneath water from a brochure. Spray
breaks on the horizon's reef and beyond that
sea a thousand metres deep. Just how
sandstone can withstand such wind
and ocean is a mystery. Just why
these walls of cliff were erected here
on unseen granite puzzles me too.
To live on an island nation is to distinguish
frontiers from boundaries. One doesn't
negotiate with oceans. I need
no visa, after lunch on our friends'
breezy veranda, to borrow their boat
and float a thousand metres over stone.

34

Another adolescence swims my way
as my daughter's friends, so many
sleek limbs, ripple like dolphins
in the sun then rise and quench

their blind nubility with a feast
of icy-creamy drinks. I remember
when my lust for highschool beauties
with Botticellian hair and a talent

for drawing horses transferred
in my second year at University
to their teachers. Now after twenty years
of teaching potential teachers

my own body's changing, losing
its comfortable contours, seeking
like those slick dolphins not to be stranded.

35

Maybe our life is an affair of coastlines
of touching on contours, of sand shifting
underfoot, of footprints straying
a shoreline. No epitaph in granite
no marble eminence, no limestone
subtlety. Tracking my prints back
is recovering tides' clean sweep
the cleansing services of storms' and winds'
abrasive erasures. The only line
that matters in the end is forward
since home is what we find when we find
what it is, they say. Still, standing on the edge
of stone seven thousand kilometres wide
my back to a whole past vivid to my eyes
I wonder why, here, it should suddenly begin.

JOHN TRANTER

I have no idea what my intentions are from day to day until I wake up. Generally I hope to live well, have fun, and write something adventurous. And I always keep this advice in mind, from a book called *Screenwriting* by Richard Walker: 'When asked to offer his single most important piece of advice for writers, writer Tommy Thompson responded after a long, thoughtful pause: Every day, no matter what else you do, get dressed.'

The Moment of Waking

She remarks how the style of a whole age
disappears into your gaze, at the moment
of waking. How sad you are
with your red shirt, your features
reminiscent of marble, your fabulous
boy-girl face like a sheet of mist
floating above a lake.

Someone hands me a ticket
In Berlin a hunchback
is printing something hideous;
my passport is bruised with dark blue
and lilac inks. Morning again,
another room batters me awake
you will be haunting the mirror like silver

Now the nights punish me with dreams
of a harbour in Italy — you are there
hung in the sky on broken wings
as you always have been, dancing,
preparing to wound me with your
distant and terrible eyes.

Lufthansa

Flying up a valley in the Alps where the rock
rushes past like a broken diorama
I'm struck by an acute feeling of precision —
the way the wing-tips flex, just a little
as the German crew adjust the tilt of the sky and
bank us all into a minor course correction
while the turbo-props gulp at the mist
with their old-fashioned thirsty thunder — or
you notice how the hostess, perfecting a smile
as she offers you a dozen drinks, enacts what is
almost a craft: Technical Drawing, for example,
a subject where desire and function, in the hands
of a Dürer, can force a thousand fine ink lines
to bite into the doubts of an epoch, spelling
Humanism. Those ice reefs repeat the motto
whispered by the snow-drifts on the north side
of the woods and model villages: the sun
has a favourite leaning, and the Nordic gloom
is a glow alcohol can fan into a flame.
And what is this truth that holds the grey
shaking metal whole while we believe in it?
The radar keeps its sweeping intermittent promises
speaking metaphysics on the phosphor screen;
our faith is sad and practical, and leads back
to our bodies, to the smile behind the drink
trolley and her white knuckles as the plane drops
a hundred feet. The sun slanting through a porthole
blitzes the ice-blocks in my glass of lemonade
and splinters light across the cabin ceiling.
No, two drinks — one for me, one for Katharina
sleeping somewhere — suddenly the Captain
lifts us up and over the final wall
explaining roads, a town, a distant lake
as a dictionary of shelter — sleeping
elsewhere, under a night sky growing bright with stars.

Glow-boys

Four a.m. At the reactor an alarm begins
howling. The core's full of shit: get out
the gloves, the phosphorescent rakes.

A burnt-out star hangs low on the horizon.
The Harrisburg glow-boys knuckle down
to work, poking around in the ashes.

They gaze out through glitter: behind the visor
putty imitates a human face, the lips
gritty, frayed, as they reach for speech

across the static field. Now a bell rings
and they wade thigh-deep into the muck,
their eyes the colour of lightning.

Five years of that and they're
too hot to touch; they wake screaming
before dawn, the pillow soaked.

What have they seen: their children's future
flare and crackle, a vast Christmas tree
flashing up from the skyline?

Rake it up, Ratshit! In a month
vacation in the Rockies, drinking rye and
blowing rattlesnakes away with a shotgun.

Now, like any cleaners, they go to work
deft and grumbling, their wives awake
in nylon nighties staring at the ceiling

and the glow of the luminous clock.
The pot of coffee popping on the stove.
The kids asleep, dreaming fitfully.

Voodoo

From his rushing-away, from his
ever-receding throne, under a rainy
canopy of trees and scraps of cloud
that topple back, shrink and disappear,
embalmed behind his rear window in a nest of
crushed velvet plush, the flash wog's nodding dog
blinks out his witless approval to the vehicles
that shadow him forever.

His twin the dipping bird sips and sips,
tilts back, cools off, dries out,
dries out utterly, totters weakly
on the lip of philosophy
then dips again.

These two critics teach us how to live,
rehearsing the gap between the no-no
and the drink-again. Their motto? Every day
I will get better at embroidering the lingo
of the tongue-tied doctors of letters; every night,
in the lack of light, I will get better
and better at the negative virtues, telling
girls to piss off, who needs them,
swimming off the edge of the rock
ledge into the plunging broth of deeper waters,
soaring up to the stratosphere, bothering the angels
and yarning with God. My left hand does it,
my right hand tells me that it's right.

In the pre-dawn rack and bash of winter peak hour
traffic on the Sydney Harbour Bridge you notice them
hefted up over the city like ju-ju dolls
in the trance of a terrible gift. You note
the man with gauntlets and the goggled girl
on motorbikes, the nurses' giggles
in the fogged-up Mini Moke, an ambulance weaving
and howling in the rear-view mirror, the tablets
rattling in the Emergency Bucket, the icy rain
furious and seething on the road, and Noddy
and his loopy brother brooding on it all
for our sake, so that we can see it whole.

Gasoline

Fabulous biting, colloquial kitty,
around the streets of the fucked-up city
I hunt for daydreams of kindness,
riding a riddle's soft punctuation.
Who taught you anal sex? Here, while
that vat of claret brews in the cellar,
let my laser restore the skin on your flanks
where the whips did their work.
Here's a rain cloud; now
drum up the suburbs of water
and paint them for me in watercolours — then
paint a gaggle of gay maidens in a giggle-buggy.
Sunk and buzzed-out in the lounge
we'll chip and chortle and chew the fat
and later, stare into this bucket of silence.
Bitter little bon-vivant factor,
country slut, we'll flick and doodle
and one tank later rise up to ecstasy then
settle the dealer's debts, Old Hand.
Oh I hear the children shrieking in this gift.

Slump, lower the heat, remembering Paris and a passion for the
raw, that scrotum dangling, which is this tale doodled and
basking in a warm audience, now a jealous shot the insult
sleeping in a mode so exactly nobody, like a working-class flirt,
with gasoline kisses — barristers dog my tracks — the Atlantic
borrowed from the Compact Disk washes up against this
memorial stone under which my brother lies exhausted in his
crimes, and still the radio, her wacky currents, unorthodox
ripples of music banging around in the dark. Salt-damp rain.
His wanton heart

Adler, Honda & Co.

It's tête-à-tête time
for the fledgelings, long dormant
under winter's mantle, now
cultivating their wits and basking
in a shabby performer's lack
of polish (likewise these politicos;
no hindrance to the leader).
Past tense, please — loose chat sprouted
to the blare of the gangster's dander,
as these gifted breathers chuckled.
Are you part of the senior set? Ah,
their drudge domain pitches and topples;
'I struggle and win,' grins the burnt-out
coma case — but he's nodding again,
scoring zero. Blacklist index, old soldiers
dozing, thievery — looming astride
the memory barrier, high-strung
like a second-rank officer, in
a narration that wanders among truck routes
the scholar rehearsed his tactics.

Hmmm, tails, looks like this batch of stuff — illuminate my
lawmaker buddy, pronto, lamps on in the blues domain —
greed network foray event, watch that uniform travesty — no
brass, no clout, but it makes an amiable evening seem like
Brazen Soldier Green Asylum neophyte reef old pal — smoky
torch glow wavers under water warehouse slope to pond —
baleful archive strongbox monograph stamped with the double
eagle

CHRIS WALLACE-CRABBE

Poetry is an art concerned with how we encounter the category of the Metaphysical, in daily practice. While it responds freshly or impressionistically to the facades and porticoes of everyday life, it keeps proffering Alec Hope's challenge, 'What questions are there that we fail to ask?' And as Mary Kinzie has memorably put its strenuous doubleness,

> Poetry subjects the indefiniteness of yearning — the yearning by which every person is encouraged to fill in the void created by living in time — to the maximum rigour, and it is rigour that makes light.

Even if a romantic or modern artistic work often exists to generate an intense yearning which can be satisfied by nothing but itself, there should be something about its formal rigour that questions the random pleasures and discomforts of the world. One works hard on the page-as-canvas; one tries to use the palette of language as richly as possible. Even in an age of diminished responsibility, the poet works towards the high calling of creating kinds of beauty. And beauty is not easy, as Beardsley said to Yeats, when asked why he created horrors. For all this, poetry can be a joyful art; it is a kind of blessing to live as a poet.

The Interval

for Peter Rose

Time out from economic bastardry
flakers on the sand
at the tail of a silly century.
The wet suits are all hanging up
like dead paratroopers; the surf
has a grumbling tummy over and over again.

Dog belts after gulls; little kids
in lairy colours canute the waves back
for a rhythmical tick, and lunch
is pathetically late as usual
for towelled blokes coming in with sandy feet.

Salty, mesmerized, a tan world is half-listening
to the accents of one-day cricket
(Henry James at the MCG, perhaps)
and one disconsolate regular shears open
a tin of beetroot. Perplexed rosellas watch.

At water's edge beige women in straw hats
rehearse gentility. Sploshing and squealing
turn out to be leggy foreplay
of the young, half in and halfway out
like stripping debutantes, or toey cattle.

Everyone's nose has grown another colour
down here, while the raunchy Xmas novel
has a dandruff of sand in its spine,
nature's form of review.
                              Time out.

Ode To Morpheus

It's a rum go, a pretty pickle, a rare kettle of fish
    that we spill so much of our time
(I will not say our days, those branchy olive intervals)
    rocking away in your arms : pointblank there.
Well, not as blank as that, but numbly a-wander
    along your tracks, your labyrinthine
halls through the great ivied house, that is
    always oneself in the long haul
studded with metamorphosis and anticlimax —
    the wide, free miniseries of the night.

It seems pretty weird, oddball, queer as a coot
    that we switch off a third of our days
swaddled in linen, squeezed between counterpane
    and kapok; perhaps under doonas.
There was a bloke in the Odd Spot who somehow got by
    on 1.5 hours per night.
Was he smarter than us? We'll never suss it out
    but I resent like crazy all of this
rehearsing for peace-without-end in our long last home.

It's a hard god, a crook umpy, a two of spades
    that figured our fortune out this way.
Instead of ranging the night we snooze in your lap,
    the years ticking away like clockwork ducks
or hurdling the fence like sheep.
                  Fiddling the hints…
    sheedling the woollen flump…
                     then, zzzz…

CHRIS WALLACE-CRABBE

Wittgenstein's Shade, 1995

Dear Gwen,
          I like to believe
that every softened evening
an austere, courteous ghost
comes in glidingly and stands
by your bed or chair,
slowly saying something like
'What God commands, that is good.'

A regular ghost,
he comes in a tweed jacket
and crumpled college slacks,
stands by you, a little stiffly,
murmuring something pretty much like
'Sound doctrines are all useless.'

I think he comes
          like a stray bird
in through your blown curtains
with his pained, patrician face,
his accent of gone Vienna,
 offering you the observation:
'the river-bed of thoughts may shift.'

You are further in
that river-bed than I am;
he returns from the other side.
His mouth has been drawn
as tight as the skin on a drum,
yet he seems quite as innocent as
the breast-feathers of a dove
and he tells you, 'It is love
that believes the resurrection.'

He will visit you, day after day.

Free Will

Your choices are dangling in the wardrobe.
They are lavender, navy or grey
as a turtledove rasping midsummer-long
by a cobbled back lane.

Your decision will haunt you,
so fraught with categories
and a thicket of repercussions:
you are in a blue funk.

What do mere shirts have to say
in a wooden world?
They feed into the shady way today
will ravel and unravel you.

A voice that is not of human origin
barracks you down to hell
or through heaven's indigo funnels of sheer depth.
It speaks you clean out of mind.

'I am,' you croak (like God himself,
without the horsepower)
but whiplash winds are dashing you now
through undreamed galaxies.

The day slides away and you fall
with a cotton torrent of laundry
into the turquoise-lacquered
Too Hard Basket.

Fight back, feathery faintheart.
It is high time to unfurl again
the enormous rippling spinnaker
of hope.

CHRIS WALLACE-CRABBE

Stardust

To a smell of water-vapour and wood fires
Walking by night, my breath allegro
To feel it's all not worth a cracker …
But how could the universe have meaning?
Would the stars be patterned differently?
The seasons vanish, or come on faster?
Would there be an End?
Perhaps we wouldn't require any sleep;
Maybe we'd no longer have to shit;
Or one radiant mathematics
Would show up trimly in everything.

Everything is just as bright
As the hollows are Indian ink
While my bones go wandering chockfull
Of a crushed silver.
These paddocks have all been marked out
With expressive diagrams
As beyond the highway ribbon
Big waves crumple and bang.

But when you ferret after the meaning
Which a universe could be hoped to have
(Oh dear, yes, one has a cold,
Or has an exam the following day,
Or on occasion has an erection,
Or they have a holiday shack up the bush)
You stick at a sort of spatial problem:
Meaning is only a bundle of signs
That parallel and light the real
But would they then be *in* the real?

Pan has left the odd footprint
On somebody's wet lawn
And his hot metallic stars
Are doing the rounds of my arteries;
I can even feel the moon
Down in my quicksilver groin,
The drypoint shadows
Falling across my brain.

Then signs are doublewise at once
Being inside and outside what they picture;
If not, they're simply beyond our ken
Like God's hand moving among the stars.
We must find a little enclosure for meaning;
It needs living room, like a dog, or a student,
And won't be satisfied with my brainpan.
I hope we can find a cosy gap
To bed it down in after all.

In those juvescent nights of starshine
When I knew what the future signified
A full moon could
Shake me with stony horror
But now it hauls me into
Pure aesthetic compliance
As a pinecone rears over its shadow
On the concrete pathway.
Such fallen silver as this
Leaches down through cracks in the earth
To take the place of marrow in ancestral bones.

ALAN WEARNE

Though definitions of poetry are a most flexible item, right now I would say it's the concentrated use of language for the enjoyment of others and yourself. That's the direction I try propelling my verse. In 1969 I wrote ... *the ultimate task of poetry ... is enjoyment ... if the poem never bores and constantly keeps the reader's wits on edge, then it could be said ... the poem is enjoyable.* I still agree.

I enjoy writing large-scale narratives and hope readers find equal pleasure. Of course I find myself having Messrs Homer, Virgil, Chaucer, Byron, Browning etc, etc, as mentors, but am even more envious of the lyric writer. Imagine how great it would be to produce a compact *Collected Poems*, nothing but one near perfect artifact after another, like Housman, like Bishop, like my late friend and colleague John Forbes.

Although I'm not a 'performance' poet I see a great deal of my work as in the oral tradition.

Any Australian poetaster complaining about their life's hard lot should read the biographies of Akhmatova, Tsvetaeva, Mandelshtam and Pasternak; and, with any humility they have, shut up. No, much better, they should attempt being about a tenth as talented as these Russians.

Oh yes and I use a computer. It's called a brain.

from Stubbsy: A Success

for Megan Jones

Money is a kind of poetry
　　　— Wallace Stevens

By the end of the 1987 fiscal year the Group had achieved its objec-
tives of achieving the long-held critical mass objective of gross assets
of $1 billion, operating businesses with a pre-eminent position in
media and entertainment and resorts and leisure in Australia and a
strong beach-head in the United States of America in the same service
industries.
　　　— Christopher Skase

… can't remember where we stood before that day,
the other mob, though, they head the ladder.
And we are towelling them. Courtesy of Iceman and
Superboot they've caught footstep fever,
Cross hasn't time to be a show pony,
and even The Moose must think he's twenty-one
and talented again.
　　　　　After every goal I knew
the cameras were back on Dix and me: it might be
one more simple Sunday arvo but this was Sunday's news:
all else around him may appear like bankrupt,
except these men: and they are playing for Stubbs!
Get him a sound bite, he'll tell you
I knew there was a hand-bag team, Australia.
Guess what? It isn't us!
　　　　　Then, by Wednesday,
with $tubb$corp stonewalling
and BoomCon still raiding like Ghengis Khan,
a diversion: the latest squib of a beat-up:
my Stags were in revolt: trying to run two truths
We're still y'mates, Craigo and the even simpler
Sorry but, can't support you.
　　　　　It had begun as an adventure:
a well-intentioned wealthmaker helping out his game.
From that day, if ever I'd the inclination,

I might try opening my mouth to yawn
Football? You must be kidding!
                            Gone were the days
of *Sure fellas sure, just put me down for the tab*
(the liquor bills, the escort fucks,
an end-of-season trip few of them deserved)
but then, as now, all they had to do was
win their mate his games and call him Craigo.
                                            Well,
he might've been staring straight in the eye of
Cyclone Ruin, that afternoon,
but some of the boys are waiting, and Stubbsy's never,
never that busy not to meet
his mighty Stags.
                    Then, as this 'deputation' seats themselves,
Pricey assumes how real livin' operates
and opens with 'Y'ratshit, Craigo... ' and how
mug-players never count for much, but just
this once, I'm to see things their way.
'What else remains?' he asks and, keeping on
with his same bait-smile, gives a reply:
'Exile with The Moose to drive you round?
Oh Craigo whoopy-doo!'
                        But few can back-pedal like me
so, after he's thanked, only a minute is required
to swing in with my final pitch:
'What you need, Shane, fellas, are facts.
Aren't you in luck: I am the CEO of facts!
And I made Moose my chauffeur?
Well who got Superboot his KFC franchise,
bought Iceman's missus her manicure salon?
And, when two of you dived into that girl's pants,
who paid off her father and the cops? More facts?
More facts! Haven't we Stags won six on-the-trot?
Aren't the punters pouring back? Aren't we set for
boom mark two? No, it'll never be time to announce
This is as good as it gets but hey,
mightn't it be a start? Sure I never played a game,
but who of you has played my game, business,
anyone?'
            Then I told about business, not real livin' business,
but the gospel according to best practice shit-kicking:
you start with jealousy, blend in hints, innuendoes,

then make your wood-duck sell and sell and sell.
I told them Fella:
'Just look down the track and see, next month,
next year, a road block named Boomer Consolidated.
Once you hit that it'll be bye-bye franchise,
oo-roo salon, evening Inspector, these are the very two.
So when you're no longer treated as sportsmen,
but mere commodities, don't come crawling home to
$tubb$corp.'
    Try smiling, Fella; it's what I said.
Whilst you're at Crazy Horse something should amuse you.
Wouldn't be Aussie, male, let's guess thirty, if it didn't
right? I'll allow it: being so drenched in the place,
by now, Stubbsy's not the man to say where novelty stops
and 'just existence' carries on.
    Months after *Sixty Minutes*
sprang us with, wouldn't you think, what went for
common knowledge, Aussie came stalking.
Him! you could almost hear them *Him!* (*Stubbs!* seeming
near impossible to say.) And then a few, well quite a few
of course, braved the idea and, with cheek or gall
or curiosity, came on in like Fella has.
    Though wouldn't you
call it 'enterprise'? I would. 'Enterprise':
what we've lacked or better never had until
a few years back. 'Enterprise': that ability to say
This one's different, sure, but since it's different
deal us in, it deserves our best.
    Can't say I invented the idea
but, round Fella's age, all I wanted to happen
I got to happen, too much sometimes.
    At $tubb$corp
press briefings grew into the art they always should be:
so *Kickbacks?* they would lob and 'Don't live in Fantasyland,'
I might return, 'Sir Joe appreciates young folk like us,
young folk giving it a go, and we, you! should appreciate
Sir Joe.'
   But only an optimist could believe
that there amongst that scrum (and didn't I say scrum?)
someone wasn't too jealous, one fella might,
with understanding, nod *Mmm not bad, making something*
of himself, giving the wide brown land more than
it deserves.

But that fella, Fella, was unlikely.
Try being Aussie and successful: all probables get
shaved back to possibles, safe possibles, safer improbables;
though take it softly, even then they'll never let you say
There's stale money: your mean, tight money,
and then there's my money: fresh money, money
that's breathing, that still can dream.
And Fella knows
they'll never let you say that, best of all, in Melbourne:
Melbourne, where the top few thousand (who think the place
is made for them) are simply losers rich enough to treat themselves
as winners, celebs who are celebs because there's always
got to be celebs. Why should they (how could they) even consider
a salesman (too much the superbox, not enough of The Members)
in short consider Stubbs?
But if a salesman has it, someone else is
sure to want it; and Melbourne did.
As money is business,
business is the world, and a salesman has to make that money
make the world.
When I started spruiking for Horizon
I jetted north half-to-all of Collins Street, the toughest of
the country's corporate cows. Old son,
I told myself, start milkin'!
And here's what I didn't say
Even though I've flown in you lot to listen
no-one's going to stride that extra mile to learn, are they?
But, since few can own today as I do,
starting now I know of two names you'll remember:
Stubbs and Horizon.
You are here now so I can ask: name that last time
you or Aussie truly dreamt,
and then made anything of that dream.
So how's about letting your money live again
here at my beach-head to paradise:
Horizon-on-Capricorn.
No, I never said quite that
but just began by aiming at their simplest pleasures:
how the rhythm of any Horizon day
began with brunch, a butler-serviced brunch,
whilst, at the Marina, Hover-Horizon
lay poised to skim away towards the Reef.
And I asked them to imagine it: a reef that holds

five hundred different kinds of fish!
                              Great pitch, Fella?
Not quite, not if you're almost over-doing it.
   Someone in the front (arms crossed, legs out)
stifled a giggle or a yawn.
'Therefore,' came his sneer, 'we're being asked to invest
in brunch, butlers, a hovercraft and, by extension, fish.'
   He waited, certain that with him
I'd taken on more than even I might handle.
Which I had, except I was going to protect my pitch
the only way I knew: by making up the rest,
adding to that, then seeing where we'd landed.
   So I tried: 'You'll invest in people at Horizon,
the real livin' dollar… ' and paused. They stared.
I shrugged and sighed:
'The Japs already have.'
                         Well not quite yet.
So I improvised this Watanabe Corporation
direct from The Ginza. Heard of the ol' one-two?
Well introducing the new:
first play your Asian card, then follow through
But Aussie money never is as good as
Jap money, is it?
                    No no no no came the panic,
we wouldn't say exactly *That*.
                         Of course they wouldn't.
   I'd known them and played them since I was
a tyro: twenty-three, heading everywhere
with a class fiancée.
                    Her old man was a journo,
who stewed these silly-buggers in his column.
Had I, he asked (raising a eyebrow,
quizzical-to-supercilious) had I heard how a former
Lord Mayor (the vascular surgeon / developer one)
bought off a union boss
(guess who if I wanted to, there'd be
no prizes) with a vein-job on the missus:
the moment she was wheeled from the theatre
concrete was cas-cading! Had I?
But let him tell me more being (quote)
Not just some crypto-pinko token-eccentric
but rather (quote again)
A clearing house for the safest, and not so safest,

313

gossip. There's one in every city, well
he was Melbourne's; which suited him:
the place was y'total amateur hour: hardly much,
correction almost nothing, ever got done. Did I know
what he would tell if he could really tell?
Why the after-hours drag queen banker
of course, the dunny-prowling prominent
back-bencher, the heiress who wasn't quite
daddy's little girl *and* their abortions but, but
This above all as Pudden his Latin Master
told him *to thine own self*... I knew the rest?
Now *That* was art and he had traded art,
well the pretence of art, for the pay cheque:
find him every weekday night inside all those Jim Geralds,
tucked under the arms of all those Jolly John Citizens
training it home to Camberwell, Moorabbin.
It got him that much extra-jaundiced,
with his tongue so firmly in his cheek
Oi ave oo alk ike iss.
                    That eyebrow raised again,
the columnist peered towards the salesman
(wouldn't 'top' Melbourne love to do without us,
well they couldn't): 'Mmm ...' he attempted,
then 'Know the only brain-fuel for this hour?
A single malt and neat. Your school Craig?'
(I named it) 'Really? That passes muster.
So who employs you?'
        I employed me: Real Livin' Toyota
of Brighton, Aspendale, Mitcham and Thornbury,
        'Mmm ... you work in car yards?'
        If it had to be described that way
well yes: I preferred 'showrooms'.

FAY ZWICKY

FAY ZWICKY

Kaddish

For my father
born 1903, died at sea, 1967

Lord of the divided, heal!

I

Father, old ocean's skull making storm calm and the waves to sleep,
Visits his first-born, humming in dreams, hiding the pearls that were
Behind *Argus*, defunct Melbourne rag. The wireless shouts declarations of

War. 'Father', says the first-born first time around (and nine years dead),
Weeping incurable for all his hidden skills. His country's Medical Journal
Laid him out amid Sigmoid Volvulus, Light on Gastric Problems, Health Services

For Young Children Yesterday Today and Tomorrow which is now and now and
now and
Never spoke his name which is Father a war having happened between her birth, his
Death: Yisborach, v'yistabach, v'yispoar, v'yisroman, v'yisnaseh — Hitler is

Dead. The Japanese are different. Let us talk of now. The war is ended.
Strangers found you first. Bearing love back, your first-born bears their praise
Into the sun-filled room, hospitals you tended, city roofs and yards, ethereal rumours.

Gray's Inn Road, Golden Square, St. George's, Birmingham, Vienna's General, the
Ancient Alfred in Commercial Road where, tearing paper in controlled strips, your
First-born waited restless and autistic, shredding life, lives, ours. 'Have to

See a patient. Wait for me,' healing knife ready as the first-born, girt to kill,
Waited, echoes of letters from Darwin, Borneo, Moratai, Brunei ('We thought him
Dead but the little Jap sat up with gun in hand and took a shot at us'), the heat

A pressing fist, swamps, insect life ('A wonderful war' said his wife who also
Waited) but wait for me wait understand O wait between the lines unread.
Your first-born did not. Tested instead the knife's weight.

*   *   *

II

Let in the strangers first: 'Apart from his high degree of medical skill he
Possessed warmth' (enough to make broken grass live? rock burst into flower?
Then why was your first-born cold?) But listen again: 'It was impossible for

Him to be rude, rough, abrupt.' Shy virgin bearing gifts to the proud first and
Only born wife, black virgin mother. Night must have come terrible to such a
Kingdom. All lampless creatures sighing in their beds, stones wailing as the

Mated flew apart in sorrow. Near, apart, fluttered, fell apart as feathered
Hopes trembled to earth shaken from the boughs of heaven. By day the heart
Was silent, shook in its box of bone, alone fathered three black dancing imps,

The wicked, the wise and the simple to jump in the house that Jack built: This
Is the priest all shaven and shorn who married the man all tattered and torn
Who kissed the maiden all forlorn who slaughtered the ox who drank the water

Who put out the fire who burnt the staff who smote the dog who bit the cat who
Ate the kid my father bought from the angel of death: 'Never heard to complain,
Response to inquiry about his health invariably brought a retort causing laughter'.

Laughter in the shadow of the fountain, laughter in the dying fire, laughter
Shaking in the box of bone, laughter fastened in the silent night, laughter
While the children danced from room to room in the empty air.

What ailed the sea that it fled? What ailed the mountains, the romping lambs
Bought with blood? Tremble, earth, before the Lord of the Crow and the Dove
Who turned flint into fountain, created the fruit of the vine devoured by the

Fox who bit the dog that worried the cat that killed the rat that ate up Jack
Who built the house: Yisgaddal v'yiskaddash sh'meh rabbo — miracle of seed,
Mystery of rain, the ripening sun and the failing flesh, courses of stars,

Stress from Sinai:
     Let (roared God)

    Great big Babylon
    Be eaten up by Persia
    Be eaten up by Greece
    Be eaten up by Rome
    Be eaten up by Ottoman
    Be eaten up by Edom
    Be eaten by Australia

317

Where Jack's house shook.

Be (Said Jack's Dad)

Submissive to an elder
Courteous to the young
Receive all men with
Cheerfulness and
Hold your tongue.

Strangers, remember Jack who did as he was told.

*   *   *

III

To the goddess the blood of all creatures is due for she gave it,
Temple and slaughterhouse, maker of curses like worm-eaten peas:

As the thunder vanishes, so shall the woman drive them away
As wax melts before flame, so let the ungodly perish before her:

She is mother of thunder, mother of trees, mother of lakes,
Secret springs, gate to the underworld, vessel of darkness,

Bearer, transformer, dark nourisher, shelterer, container of
Living and dead, coffin of Osiris, dark-egg devourer, engenderer,

Nurturer, nurse of the world, many-armed goddess girdled by cobras,
Flame-spewer, tiger-tongued queen of the dead and the violent dancers.

Mother of songs, dancer of granite, giver of stone —
Let his wife speak:

'Honour thy father and thy mother'
So have I done and done and done — no marriage shall ever

Consume the black maidenhead — my parents are heaven
Bound. I shall rejoin them;

Bodies of men shall rejoin severed souls
At the ultimate blast of invisible grace.

Below, I burn,
Naomi of the long brown hair, skull in a Juliet cap.

Do the dead rot? Then rot as I rot as they rot,
'Honour thy Father' sing Armistice bells, *espressivo*.

The stumbling fingers are groping
To pitch of perfection.

I am that pitch
I am that perfection.

Papa's a civilian again, mother is coiled in a corset,
Dispenses perfection with:

Castor oil
Tapestry
Tablecloths (white)
Rectal thermometers
Czerny and prunes
Sonatinas of Hummel
The white meat of chicken
The white meat of fish
The maids and the lost silver.

Lord, I am good for nothing, shall never know want.

Blinded, I burn, am led not into temptation.

The home is the centre of power.
                              There I reign
Childless. Three daughters, all whores, all —

Should be devoured by the fires of Gehenna
Should be dissolved in the womb that bore them
Should wander the wastelands forever.

Instead, they dance.

Whole towns condemn me. Flames from the roofs
Form my father's fiery image. He waves, laughs,

Cools his head among stars, leaves me shorn,
Without sons, unsanctified, biting on

Bread of affliction. Naked, I burn,
Orphaned again in a war.

The word is a different oyster:
Mine.

His defection will not be forgotten.

*   *   *

IV

Blessed be He whose law speaks of the three different characters of children who
we are to instruct on this occasion:

What says the wicked one?

'What do you all mean by this?'
This thou shalt ask not, for thou has transgressed, using *you* and
excluding thyself.

Thou shalt not exclude thyself from:

The collective body of the family
The collective body of the race
The collective body of the nation

Therefore repeat after me:

'This is done because of what the Eternal did
For me when I came forth from Egypt.'

The wicked wants always the last word (for all the good
It does): 'Had I been there, I would still not be worth

My redemption'. Nothing more may be eaten, a beating will
Take place in the laundry. Naked.
'Honour thy father and thy mother'

What says the wise one?

'The testimonies, statutes, the judgments delivered by God
I accept'.

Nonetheless, though thou are wise,
After the paschal offering there shall be no dessert.

'Honour thy father and thy mother'

What says the simple one?

Asks merely: 'What is this?'
Is told: 'With might of hand

Did our God bring us forth out of Egypt
From the mansion of bondage.'

Any more questions? Ask away and be damned.

'Honour thy father and thy mother'

Yisborach, v'yistabach, v'yispoar, v'yisroman, v'yisnaseh, v'yishaddor,
v'yisalleh, v'yishallol, sh'meh d'kudsho, b'rich hu

Praise death who is our God
Live for death who is our God
Die for death who is our God
Blessed be your failure which is our God

Oseh sholom bim'romov, hu yaaseh sholom, olenu v'al kol yisroel, v'imru Omen.

*   *   *

V

And he who was never born and cannot inquire shall say:

There is a time to speak
and a time to be silent
There is a time to forgive
And a time in which to be
Forgiven.
After forgiveness,

Silence.

BIOGRAPHIES AND PUBLICATIONS

Robert Adamson, born in 1943, successfully combines the careers of poet, editor and publisher. He was instrumental in creating and editing *New Poetry* magazine and Prism Books. He lives on the Hawkesbury where, with Juno Gemes, he directs and edits Paper Bark Press for Craftsman House. His book *The Clean Dark* (1990), won Australia's major poetry awards: the Kenneth Slessor Award (The New South Wales Literary Awards), the Turnbull Fox Phillips Poetry Prize (the National Book Council's Banjo Awards) and the C J Dennis Prize (the Victorian Premier's Literary Awards). His autobiographical *Wards of the State* was shortlisted in 1992 for the *Age* Book of the Year. He is currently contributing editor to *Boxkite*. His book, *Waving to Hart Crane*, was awarded the Christopher Brennan Award in 1996.

Canticles on the Skin Illumination Press, 1970.
Swamp Riddles Island Press, 1973.
Cross the Border Prism, 1975.
Where I Come From Big Smoke Books, 1979.
The Law at Heart's Desire Prism, 1982.
Selected Poems 1970-1989 UQP, 1989.
The Clean Dark Paper Bark Press, 1990.
Waving to Hart Crane Angus & Robertson, 1994.
The Language of Oysters Craftsman House, 1997.
Meaning Poetical Histories, 1998.
Black Water Brandl & Schlesinger, 1999.

Adam Aitken is assistant editor for *HEAT* magazine. Born in London, he attended various schools in Thailand and Malaysia before settling in Sydney. He has read his work in Hawaii, published widely in Australia, and is a two-time winner of the Australian Sports Poem Award. Recently he was awarded an ASIALINK writer's residency in Malaysia.

Letter to Marco Polo Island Press, 1985.
In One House Angus & Robertson/Paper Bark Press, 1996.
Crossing Lake Toba Folio(Salt), 1998.

Lisa Bellear (Goernpil) is a writer, visual artist, academic, radio broadcaster and social commentator. Actively involved in Indigenous affairs, she is an executive member of the Black Women's Action in Education Foundation (BWAEF), and has sat on the Aboriginal and Torres Strait Islander Literature Panel of the Australia Council, and the selection committee of the RAKA (Ruth Adney Koori) Award. She has read her poetry in literary festivals, pubs and conferences and has been published in many journals and anthologies. She currently lives in Melbourne and is completing a Masters in Creative Writing at the University of Queensland.

Dreaming in Urban Areas UQP, 1996.

Judith Beveridge was born in England in 1956 and came to Australia in 1960. She has won the Mary Gilmore Award and the NSW and Victorian Premiers' Prizes. She was co-founder of the poetry journal *Hobo*.

The Domesticity of Giraffes Black Lightning Press, 1987.
Accidental Grace UQP, 1996.

Ken Bolton was born in 1949. Formerly of Sydney, he has lived in Adelaide since 1982 where he is associated with the Experimental Art Foundation. His *Two Poems — a drawing of the sky* was shortlisted for the Victorian Premier's Poetry Prize in 1991. In 1992 his manuscript collection *The Westbury Street Poems* won the Wesley Michel Wright Prize. He edits *Otis Rush* magazine and Little Esther books (web site: http://www.eaf.asn.au/otisrush.html). His art criticism has appeared in many Australian art magazines.

Four Poems Sea Cruise Books, 1977.
Blonde & French Island Press, 1977.
Christ's Entry into Brussels, or Ode to the Three Stooges Red Press, 1978.
Two Sestinas beer rhymes with bier press, 1980.
Talking To You, Rigmarole, 1983.
Blazing Shoes Open Dammit, 1984.
Notes For Poems Shocking Looking Books, 1984.
Two Poems — a drawing of the sky Experimental Art Foundation, 1990.
Sestina to the Centre of the Brain Little Esther, 1991.
Selected Poems, 1975–1990 Penguin, 1992.
'Untimely Meditations' & other poems, Wakefield Press, 1997.

Airborne Dogs (with John Jenkins), Brunswick Hills Press, 1988.
The Ferrara Poems (with John Jenkins), Experimental Art
    Foundation, 1989.
The Gutman Variations (with John Jenkins), Little Esther, 1993.

Peter Boyle was born in Melbourne in 1951. He attended high school
in Sydney and went on to Sydney University where he was a contemporary of the late John Forbes. In the seventies and eighties he
wrote several prose works as well as some poetry, most of which is
unpublished. From the late eighties he has concentrated on poetry.
His first book, *Coming Home From the World*, won the NSW Premier's
Award as well as the National Book Council Banjo Award. His
second book, *The Blue Cloud of Crying*, also won the Banjo Award and
the Adelaide Festival Poetry Prize.

Coming Home From the World Five Islands Press, 1994.
The Blue Cloud of Crying Hale & Iremonger, 1997.

Pam Brown was born in Victoria. She has lived, at times, in Brisbane,
Toowoomba, Melbourne and Adelaide — always returning, in her
adult life, to Sydney, where she currently lives with her partner. She
has travelled to Asia, Europe, and the Pacific. She has been involved
in video and film making, a rock band, theatre, screen-printing and
political activism. She has held various jobs, and since 1990 has
worked in a sciences library at the University of Sydney. She is the
poetry editor for *overland* magazine.

Sureblock Pat Woolley, 1972.
Cocabola's Funny Picture Book Tomato Press, 1973.
Automatic Sad Tomato Press, 1974.
Cafe Sport Sea Cruise Books, 1979.
Correspondences (with Joanne Burns) Red Press, 1979.
Country & Eastern Never-Never Books, 1980.
Small Blue View EAF/Magic Sam, 1982.
Selected Poems Wild & Woolley, 1984.
Keep It Quiet Sea Cruise Books, 1987.
New & Selected Poems Wild & Woolley, 1990.
Little Droppings Never-Never Books, 1994.
This World. This Place. UQP, 1994.
50–50 Little Esther, 1997.

joanne burns is a writer of poetry, prose poems, short fiction and monologues. Her work has been widely published and performed. She lives in Sydney.

Snatch Strange Faeces, 1972.
Ratz Saturday Centre, 1973.
Adrenalin Flicknife Saturday Centre, 1976.
Radio City 2 am (with Stephanie Bennett and Ruth K Fordam) Cochon, 1977.
Correspondences (with Pamela Brown) Red Press, 1979.
ventriloquy Sea Cruise Books, 1981.
blowing bubbles in the 7th lane FAB Press, 1988.
on a clear day UQP, 1992; now ETT IMPRINT.
penelope's knees UQP, 1996.
aerial photography Five Islands Press, 1999.

Caroline Caddy was born in Western Australia in 1944 and spent significant periods of her childhood in the United States of America and Japan. She has lived on small properties on the south coast of Western Australia and is now growing olives in the area. She has raised two children and won the Western Australia Week Literary Award for Poetry, and the National Book Council Award for poetry in 1992.

Singing at Night Fremantle Arts Centre Press, 1980
Letters from the North Fremantle Arts Centre Press, 1985
Beach Plastic Fremantle Arts Centre Press, 1989
Conquistadors Penguin, 1991
Antarctica Fremantle Arts Centre Press, 1996.
Working Temple Fremantle Arts Centre Press, 1997.
Editing the Moon Fremantle Arts Centre Press, 1999.

Alison Clark is a Jungian therapist living in Sydney. She has taught Italian at Sydney University, and worked for Macquarie Dictionary and SBS Subtitles. She is married with three grown-up children.

Ananke Scripsi, 1987.
About Desire Heinemann, 1996.

Alison Croggon's poetry has been published widely in anthologies and magazines in Australia and overseas. Her first book of poems, *This is the Stone*, won the Anne Elder and Dame Mary Gilmore Prizes. Her novel *Navigatio* was highly commended in the 1995 *Australian*/Vogel literary award. Her second book of poems, *The Blue Gate*, was released in 1997. Her work for theatre includes opera and music theatre. She was poetry editor for *Overland Extra* (1992), *Modern Writing* (1992-1994) and *Voices* (1996). Her critical work has appeared in *The Bulletin*, *The Age*, *Quadrant*, *Voices* and on ABC radio and television, and she edits *Masthead* literary arts magazine.

This is the Stone Penguin, 1991.
The Blue Gate Black Pepper Press, 1997.

M T C Cronin's work has appeared in New Zealand, the United Kingdom, Europe, Canada and the United States, as well as her native Australia. Born in Merriwa in the Hunter Valley area of New South Wales and raised in Caloundra on the Queensland coast, she now resides in Sydney. In 1997 she won the Gwen Harwood Memorial Poetry Prize and in 1998 was awarded a Marten Bequest Travelling Scholarship to travel overseas and work on a manuscript of poetry.

Zoetrope — we see us moving Five Islands Press, 1995.
Everything Holy Balcones International Press, 1998.
The World Beyond The Fig Five Islands Press, 1998.
Bestseller Hazard Press, 1999.

Sarah Day was born in Upholland, England. Her family emigrated to Australia while she was still a child. She lives in Hobart where she is poetry editor for *Island*. She has two young daughters, is at present working on a state government literature grant and is a member of the Literature Fund of the Australia Council. She has won the Anne Elder Award and was resident at the Australia Council Studio in Rome in 1993.

A Hunger To Be Less Serious Angus & Robertson, 1987.
A Madder Dance Penguin, 1992.
Quickening Penguin, 1997.

Laurie Duggan was born in Melbourne in 1949. He studied at Monash and Sydney Universities, and recently completed a PhD in Fine Arts at the University of Melbourne. He has worked as a lecturer in media, as a screenwriter and art critic, and was recently the poetry editor of *Meanjin*. He has published ten books of poems and his work has appeared in several anthologies. In 1987 he took part in an Australia Council-sponsored reading tour of the United States and Canada, and in 1992 he was a guest at the Wellington Festival of Arts. As the result of his doctoral research he hopes to publish a work on imagined space in early twentieth-century Australian visual arts.

East: Poems 1970–74 Rigmarole, 1976.
Under The Weather Wild & Woolley, 1978.
Adventures in Paradise Experimental Art Foundation, 1982; Little Esther, 1991.
The Great Divide: Poems 1973–83 Hale & Iremonger, 1985.
The Ash Range Pan/Picador, 1987.
The Epigrams of Martial Scripsi, 1989.
Blue Notes Pan/Picador, 1990.
The Home Paddock Noone's Press, 1991.
Memorials Little Esther, 1996.
New and Selected Poems, 1971–1993 UQP, 1996.

Diane Fahey was born in Melbourne and now lives by the sea in country Victoria. Her poetry is published internationally, and she has given poetry readings in Europe and the United States, as well as at many venues in Australia. She has received various writers' fellowships and grants from the Australia Council, and the South Australian and Victorian governments, and is currently the recipient of a three-year New Work Grant from the Literature Fund of the Australia Council. Among her numerous poetry prizes are the Mattara Poetry Prize and the Wesley Michel Wright Poetry Prize. *Metamorphoses* was shortlisted for the Victorian and NSW Premiers 'Awards in 1988; and *Mayflies in Amber* was shortlisted for the Adelaide Festival Awards in 1994. She was writer-in-residence at the University of Adelaide in 1997, and at Ormond College, University of Melbourne, in 1994, and is a fellow of Hawthornden International Writers' Centre.

Voices from the Honeycomb Jacaranda, 1996.
Metamorphoses Dangaroo, 1988.
Turning the Hourglass Dangaroo, 1990.

Mayflies in Amber Angus & Robertson/HarperCollins, 1993.
The Body in Time Spinifex, 1995.
Listening to a Far Sea Hale & Iremonger, 1998.

Lionel Fogarty was born on the land of the Wakka Wakka tribe at Barambah, Queensland, now known as the Cherbourg Aboriginal Reserve. His poetry grew out of both a commitment to the Aboriginal cause and also a desire to communicate the traditional ways and beliefs of his community. Over the years, his writing has been informed by a wealth of experience as an activist, tribal member and a father. Although he has now published several books of poetry, he regards himself as a 'speaker' rather than a 'writer'.

Kargun Murri Cooee, 1980.
Yoogum Yoogum Penguin, 1982.
Kudjela Murri Cooee, 1983.
Ngutji Murri Cooee, 1984.
Jagera Murri Cooee, 1990.
New and Selected Poems: Munaldjali, Mutuerjaraera Hyland House, 1995.

John Forbes was in many ways a metaphysical poet of the late twentieth century. He was born in Melbourne in 1950 and died there in January 1998. He studied at the University of Sydney, worked as a furniture removalist and creative writing teacher, and was founding editor of the occasional journal *Surfers Paradise*. He had a profound knowledge of poetry and a brilliant intellect. His influence extended beyond the world of poetry into contemporary Australian cultural debate. Showing much affection for the society he ironised in his verse, he was equally capable of being self-critical. Though definitively the 'Australian poet', his work fits into an international context. Influenced by the New York School of poets, he remained a devotee of the work of Frank O'Hara and John Ashbery. A sharp critic, and a sparkling conversationalist, he will live forever in the memory of his friends and students.

Ode to Tropical Skiing Angus & Robertson, 1976.
On The Beach Sea Cruise Books, 1977.
Drugs Black Lamb Press, 1979.
Stalin's Holidays Transit Poetry, 1981.

The Stunned Mullet Hale & Iremonger, 1988.
New and Selected Poems Angus & Robertson, 1992.
Troubador Folio, 1993.
Humidity Equipage, UK, 1998.
Damaged Glamour Brandl & Schlesinger, 1998.

Peter Goldsworthy's first collection of poetry, *Readings From Ecclesiastes*, won the Commonwealth Poetry Prize, the Anne Elder Award and the South Australian Biennial Literary Award. His second collection, *This Goes With This*, was awarded, jointly, the Australian Bicentennial Poetry Prize. He wrote the libretto for the Richard Mills' opera *Summer of the Seventeenth Doll*, based on Ray Lawler's play, and is working on another libretto with Mills for the Australian Opera, for the year 2000. His novels and poetry have been translated into many European and Asian languages.

Readings From Ecclesiastes Angus & Robertson, 1982.
This Goes With That ABC, 1988.
This Goes With This: Selected Poems 1970-1991 Angus & Robertson, 1991.
After the Ball National Library of Australia, 1992.
If, Then HarperCollins, 1997.

Robert Gray was born in 1945 and grew up on the far north coast of New South Wales where his father owned a banana plantation. After working on a country newspaper as a journalist Gray moved to Sydney at the age of nineteen where he has since worked as a reviewer, editor, advertising copywriter, and a buyer for book-shops. Gray's many awards include the NSW and Victorian Premiers' Awards for poetry, the Patrick White Award, and numerous fellowships from the Australia Council. He has been writer-in-residence at a number of Australian universities and at Meiji University in Tokyo. He is the editor of the *Selected Poems* of Shaw Neilson and has co-edited — with Geoffrey Lehmann — two anthologies: *The Younger Australian Poets* and *Australian Poetry in the Twentieth Century*.

Creekwater Journal Angus & Robertson, 1973.
Grass Script Angus & Robertson, 1978.
The Skylight Angus & Robertson, 1983.
Piano Angus & Robertson, 1988.

Certain Things Heinemann, 1993.
Lineations Duffy & Snellgrove, 1996.
Selected Poems Duffy & Snellgrove, 1998.

J S Harry was born in South Australia but now lives in Sydney. Her various jobs have included educational bookselling and editing the ABC Radio National's 'First Hearing' program. She has also been writer-in-residence at the Australian National University. Her awards include the Harri Jones Memorial Prize, the PEN International Lyne Phillips Prize, and the NSW Premier's Prize.

the deer under the skin UQP, 1971.
Hold, for a Little While, and Turn Gently Island Press, 1979.
A Dandelion for Van Gogh Island Press, 1985.
The Life on Water and the Life Beneath Angus & Robertson/Paper Bark Press, 1995.
Selected Poems Penguin, 1995.

Kevin Hart has published six volumes of poetry and three works of literary criticism. He is the editor of *The Oxford Book of Australian Religious Verse* (1994), and the translator of *The Buried Harbour: Selected Poems of Giuseppe Ungaretti* (Leros, 1991). He is Professor of English and Comparative Literature at Monash University and lives in Melbourne with his wife and two children.

New and Selected Poems HarperCollins, 1995.
Dark Angel Dedalus Press, 1996.
The Trespass of the Sign Cambridge University Press, 1990.
A D Hope Oxford University Press, 1992.
Samuel Johnson and the Culture of Property Cambridge University Press, 1999.
Wicked Heat Paper Bark Press/Craftsman House, 1999.

Dennis Haskell is a poet, critic and editor who teaches at the University of Western Australia. He has been an editor of the literary magazine *Westerly* since 1985, was for three years the poetry critic for 'Books and Writing', and has published twelve books — including studies of John Keats, Kenneth Slessor and Australian poetic satire.

He was once an accountant and thus feels that he has made a double entry into life. Somehow he seems driven to fear the Jabberwocky of idleness.

Listening at Night Angus & Robertson, 1984.
A Touch of Ginger (with Fay Zwicky) Folio, 1992.
Abracadabra Fremantle Arts Centre Press, 1993.
The Ghost Names Sing Fremantle Arts Centre Press, 1997.

Dorothy Hewett was born in Perth, Western Australia in 1923. She is married to the writer Merv Lilley, has five children and lives in the Blue Mountains outside Sydney. In addition to her poetry, she has published two novels, an autobiography and thirteen plays, as well as many articles and short stories.

What About the People! (with Merv Lilley) Realist Writers, 1963.
Hidden Journey Wattle Grove Press, 1967.
Late Night Bulletin Wattle Grove Press, 1968.
Windmill Country Overland, 1968.
Rapunzel in Suburbia Prism, 1975.
Greenhouse Big-Smoke Books, 1979.
Alice in Wormland Paper Bark Press, 1987.
A Tremendous World in Her Head Dangaroo Press, 1989
Selected Poems Fremantle Arts Centre Press, 1991.
Peninsula Fremantle Arts Centre Press, 1994.
Collected Poems 1940–1995, Fremantle Arts Centre Press, 1995.

Coral Hull was born in Paddington, New South Wales in 1965. She is a full-time writer and a member of The Field Naturalists Club of Victoria and The Australian Society of Authors. She is an animal rights advocate and the Director of Animal Watch Australia, an online publishers' directory and resource site on animal rights and vegetarian issues. She completed a Master of Arts Degree at Deakin University in 1994 and a Doctor of Creative Arts Degree at the University of Wollongong in 1998. Her work has been published extensively in literary magazines in the USA, Canada, Australia and the United Kingdom.

In The Dog Box of Summer in *Hot Collation* Penguin, 1995.
William's Mongrels in *The Wild Life* Penguin, 1996.

Broken Land Five Islands Press, 1997.
How Do Detectives Make Love? Penguin, 1998.

S K Kelen was born the year the Olympics and television came to Australia and grew up in Sydney. He started writing in 1970 and first published in *Poetry Australia* in 1973. Since then, his work has been published widely in Australia and overseas. He has worked in many professions, including mail sorter, storeman and packer, brewery labourer, librarian, public servant, speech writer, and creative writing teacher. He lives with his family in Canberra and enjoys travelling.

The Gods Ash Their Cigarettes Makar Press, 1978.
To the Heart of the World's Electricity Senor Press, 1980.
Atomic Ballet Hale & Iremonger, 1991.
Dingo Sky Angus & Robertson, 1993.
West of Krakatoa Limestone Press, 1994.
Trans-Sumatran Highway and other poems Polonius, 1995.
Dragon Rising Thé' Giói Publishers, Hanoi, 1998.

John Kinsella was born in Perth in 1963. He studied at the University of Western Australia and travelled extensively through Europe, the Middle East, and Asia. He has published poems in literary journals internationally and has received several writing grants. In 1996 he received a Young Australian Creative Fellowship, and he was awarded a two-year Fellowship from the Literature Fund of the Australia Council. He was made an artist By-Fellow of Churchill College, Cambridge in 1997 and a Fellow in 1998. He is the founding editor of the literary magazine *Salt* and co-editor of *Stand* in the United Kingdom. His fiction includes a novel, *Genre*, and a collection of short stories, *Grappling Eros.*

The Frozen Sea Zeppelin Press, 1983.
The Book of Two Faces PICA, 1989.
Night Parrots Fremantle Arts Centre Press, 1989.
Eschatologies Fremantle Arts Centre Press, 1991.
Full Fathom Five Fremantle Arts Centre Press, 1993.
Syzygy Fremantle Arts Centre Press, 1993.
The Silo: A Pastoral Symphony Fremantle Arts Centre Press, 1995, Arc, UK, 1996.
Erratum/Frame(d) Folio/Fremantle Arts Centre Press, 1995.

The Radnoti Poems Equipage, United Kingdom, 1996.
Anathalamion Poetical Histories, United Kingdom, 1996.
The Undertow: New and Selected Poems Arc, UK, 1996.
Lightning Tree Fremantle Arts Centre Press, 1996.
Poems 1980–1994 Fremantle Arts Centre Press, 1997.
Graphology Equipage, UK, 1997.
The Hunt Fremantle Arts Centre Press, 1998.
Kangaroo Virus Folio/Fremantle Arts Centre Press, 1998.
Visitants Bloodaxe Books, UK, 1999.

Anthony Lawrence lives in Hobart. His work has been published widely in Australia and overseas, and his many awards include the inaugural Gwen Harwood Memorial Prize, the 1997 New South Wales Premier's Award, and the 1997 Newcastle Poetry Prize. His first novel *Wakelines* is forthcoming, and a play, *The Boneyard*, co-written with Mark O'Flynn, is to premiere at Melbourne's LaMama Theatre in 1999.

Dreaming in Stone Angus & Robertson, 1989.
Three Days out of Tidal Town Hale & Iremonger, 1991.
The Darkwood Aquarium Penguin, 1993.
Cold Wires of Rain Penguin, 1994.
The Viewfinder UQP, 1996.
Skinned by Light: New & Selected Poems UQP, 1998.

Rhyll McMaster was born in 1947 and has been writing and publishing poetry since she was sixteen. Her books have been short listed for most of the major awards and have won prizes such as the Harri Jones Memorial Prize, the Victorian Premier's Prize and the Grace Leven Prize. She has twice been the recipient of grants from the Literature Board of the Australia Council and was the first poet to win the CAPO Fellowship from the Capital Art Patrons' Organisation, ACT, in 1997. She has performed many public readings and lectures. Her most ambitious project to date was a two-hour show called Hard & Soft, with a four-piece band and singer incorporating her poetry and blues and pop songs from the sixties, performed in 1997 at Tilley's Cafe, ACT.

The Brineshrimp UQP, 1972.
Washing The Money, Poems with Photographs Angus & Robertson, 1986.
On My Empty Feet William Heinemann, 1993.

Flying The Coop: New and Selected Poems 1972–1994 William
    Heinemann, 1994.
Evolutionary History of Edward Kelly in Primary Colours Nolan Gallery,
    ACT, 1997.
Chemical Bodies Brandl & Schlesinger, 1997.

Jennifer Maiden was born in Penrith, New South Wales, in 1949. She
has a Bachelor of Arts degree from Macquarie University and is a
professional writer with fourteen published books, including two
novels, many essays and reviews. Her poetry collection, *The Winter
Baby*, won both the New South Wales and Victorian Premiers'
Awards in 1991. The 'Gulf War' sequence and the long, two-voice
narrative 'Guarding the Cenotaph', from her latest collection *Acoustic
Shadow*, were broadcast on Radio National. Her novel *Play With
Knives* has been translated and published in Germany by dtv. She has
a twelve-year-old daughter, Katharine. Her next collection *Mines* is
due out from Paper Bark Press in 1999.

Tactics UQP, 1974.
The Problem of Evil Prism, 1975.
The Occupying Forces Gargoyle, 1975.
Mortal Details Rigmarole of the Hours, 1977.
Birthstones Angus & Robertson, 1978.
The Border Loss Angus & Robertson, 1979.
For the Left Hand South Head Press, 1981.
The Terms Hale & Iremonger, 1982.
The Trust Black Lightning, 1988.
Selected Poems Penguin, 1990.
Play with Knives Allen & Unwin, 1990.
The Winter Baby Angus & Robertson, 1990.
Bastille Day National Library of Australia, 1990.
Acoustic Shadow Penguin, 1993.

Peter Minter was born in 1967. He was a founding editor of *Cordite
Poetry* and *Poetics Review*, and was editor of the *Varuna New Poetry*
broadsheet. His first volume of poems was shortlisted for the NSW
Premier's Prize for Poetry, and his recent publications include a wide
range of work in Australian and international publications. At
present he is a contributing editor to *Boxkite* and, with Michael
Brennan, is collating *Terra Nova*, an anthology of new and innovative
Australian poetry.

Rhythm in a Dorsal Fin Five Islands Press, 1995.
Empty Texas – a Selection, Folio(Salt), UK, 1998.
Empty Texas Paper Bark Press/Craftsman House, 1999.

Les Murray lives in Bunyah in New South Wales, where he was born in 1938. After studying at Sydney University and working as a linguist, he retired to full-time writing in 1971. He is editor of the *New Oxford Book of Australian Verse* and has published his selected prose in *A Working Forest* Duffy & Snellgrove, 1998.

The Ilex Tree (with Geoffrey Lehmann) ANU Press, 1965.
The Weatherboard Cathedral Angus & Robertson, 1969.
Poems Against Economics Angus & Robertson, 1972.
Lunch And Counter Lunch Angus & Robertson, 1974.
Ethnic Radio Angus & Robertson, 1977.
The People's Otherworld Angus & Robertson, 1983.
The Daylight Moon Angus & Robertson, 1987.
Dog Fox Field Angus & Robertson, 1990.
Translations From The Natural World Isabella Press, 1992.
Subhuman Redneck Poems Duffy & Snellgrove, 1996.
Fredy Neptune Duffy & Snellgrove, 1998.
New and Selected Poems Duffy & Snellgrove, 1998.

Geoff Page is a Canberra poet who has published eleven books of poetry, two novels, a biography, a book of short stories and poems and edited two anthologies. With time off for occasional short grants or residencies he has worked full-time running the English department at Narrabundah College in the ACT since 1974. He has read and talked on poetry in Bern, Beijing, London, Lecce, Bologna, Guangzhou and Singapore. He has been writer in residence at Wollongong University, the Australian Defence Force Academy, Curtin University and Edith Cowan University.

The Question UQP, 1971.
Smalltown Memorials UQP, 1975.
Collecting the Weather Makar Press, 1978.
Cassandra Paddocks Angus & Robertson, 1983.
Clairvoyant in Winter Angus & Robertson, 1980.
Collected Lives Angus & Robertson, 1986.
Smiling in English, Smoking in French Brindabella Officina, 1987.
Footwork Angus & Robertson, 1988.
Invisible Histories Picador, 1990.

Selected Poems Angus & Robertson, 1991.
Gravel Corners Angus & Robertson, 1992.
Human Interest William Heinemann Australia, 1994.
A Reader's Guide to Contemporary Australian Poetry UQP, 1995.
Mrs Schnell Arrives in Heaven and Other Light Verse Polonius Press, 1995.
The Great Forgetting (with Bevan Hayward) (Pooaraar) Aboriginal Studies Press, 1996.
The Secret William Heinemann, 1997.
Bernie McGann: A Life in Jazz Kardoorair Press, 1997.
Collateral Damage Indigo, 1999.
The Scarring Hale & Iremonger, 1999.

Dorothy Porter was born in Sydney in 1954. She has published five books of poetry, three verse novels and two novels for young adults. Her crime thriller in verse, *The Monkey's Mask*, won the *Age* Poetry Book of the Year Award and the National Book Council Banjo Award for Poetry, and was shortlisted for the NSW State Literary Awards, the Booksellers' Book of the Year and the Australian Literature Society's Gold Medal. In 1997, a United Kingdom edition of *The Monkey's Mask* was published by Serpent's Tail and nominated as one of the Best Books of the Year in *The Times*. *The Monkey's Mask* is now one of the fastest-selling works of poetry ever published in Australia. *Crete*, her first collection of poetry since 1989, was shortlisted for the 1996 National Book Council Banjo Awards and the Colin Roderick Award 1997. She now lives in Melbourne.

Little Hoodlum Prism, 1975.
Bison Prism, 1979.
The Night Parrot Black Lightning Press, 1984.
Driving Too Fast UQP, 1989; second edition, Hyland House, 1996.
Crete Hyland House, 1996.
Akhenaten UQP, 1992; second edition, Hyland House, 1998.
The Monkey's Mask Hyland House, 1994.
What a Piece of Work Picador, 1999.

Peter Porter was born in Brisbane in 1929. Educated in Brisbane and Toowoomba during the Second World War, he moved to London in 1951 where he has lived ever since. He has published sixteen original books of verse plus four more with pictures by Arthur Boyd. Since 1968 he has been a freelance reviewer, critic and broadcaster, specialising in poetry and music — and would like to branch out into his latest enthusiasm, European painting. He and his second wife, who have four daughters and eight grandchildren between them, live in Central London, where the prices will soon drive them out. He revisits Australia frequently and is the editor of *The Oxford Book of Modern Australian Verse* (1996).

Once Bitten, Twice Bitten Scorpion Press, 1961.
Penguin Modern Poets, No. 2 Penguin, 1962.
Poems Ancient & Modern Scorpion Press, 1964.
Words Without Music Sycamore Press, 1968.
Solemn Adultery at Breakfast Creek: An Australian Ballad (with Michael Jessett) Keepsake Press, 1968.
A Porter Folio Scorpion Press, 1969.
The Last of England Oxford University Press, 1970.
Preaching to the Converted Oxford University Press, 1972.
After Martial Oxford University Press, 1972.
A Share of the Market Ulsterman Publications, 1973.
Jonah (with Arthur Boyd) Secker & Warburg, 1973.
The Lady and the Unicorn (with Arthur Boyd) Secker & Warburg, 1975.
Living in a Calm Country Oxford University Press, 1975.
Les Très Riches Heures Keepsake Press, 1978.
The Cost of Seriousness Oxford University Press, 1978.
English Subtitles Oxford University Press, 1981.
The Animal Programme Anvil Press, 1982.
Covent Garden Celebratory Ode Friends of Covent Garden, 1982.
Collected Poems Oxford University Press, 1983.
Fast Forward Oxford University Press, 1984.
Narcissus (with Arthur Boyd) Secker & Warburg, 1984.
The Run of Your Father's Library Albion Press, Leeds University, 1984.
Machines Starwheel Press, 1986.
The Automatic Oracle Oxford University Press, 1987.
Mars (with Arthur Boyd) André Deutsch, 1988.
A Porter Selected Oxford University Press, 1989.
Possible Worlds Oxford University Press, 1989.
The Chair of Babel Oxford University Press, 1992.
Millennial Fables Oxford University Press, 1994.
Dragons in their Pleasant Palaces Oxford University Press, 1997.
Collected Poems (1961-1999) Oxford University Press, 1999, 2 vols.

Peter Rose grew up in northern Victoria and did an arts degree at Monash University. After some years as a medical bookseller he moved into publishing in 1986. He is now the Trade and Reference Publisher at Oxford University Press in Melbourne. His work has appeared in various anthologies and journals.

The House of Vitriol Picador, 1990.
The Catullan Rag Picador, 1993.
Donatello in Wangaratta Hale & Iremonger, 1998.

Gig Ryan lives in Melbourne where she is poetry editor for *The Age*. She has won the Anne Elder Poetry Award and has received fellowships from the Literature Board of the Australia Council. She is also a writer-singer, formerly with Disband, who released 'Six Goodbyes' (1988), and now with Driving Past, CD 'Real Estate' (1999).

The Division of Anger Transit Press, 1981.
Manners of an Astronaut Hale & Iremonger, 1984.
The Last Interior Scripsi, 1986.
Excavation PanPicador Australia, 1990.
Research Folio(Salt), UK, 1998.
Pure And Applied Paper Bark Press/Craftsman House, 1998.

Tracy Ryan was born in Western Australia but now lives in England, where she has worked as a bookseller, tutor, writer and Judith E Wilson Junior Visiting Fellow at Robinson College, Cambridge. She has published poetry and fiction.

Killing Delilah Fremantle Arts Centre Press, 1994.
Bluebeard in Drag Fremantle Arts Centre Press, 1996.
Slant rempress, 1997.
The Willing Eye Fremantle Arts Centre Press, 1999.

Philip Salom was born in Western Australia in 1950. He has twice won the Commonwealth Poetry Prize, awarded in London, the Western Australian Premier's Award for Poetry three times, and has had several shortlistings for the Victorian Premier's Prize and the National Book Council Poetry Award. In 1996 his poem 'Elegy for My Father' won the Newcastle Poetry Prize. He also writes fiction and literary reviews and is developing work for CD ROM and the internet. He has been a guest reader in the United States, Canada, the United Kingdom, the former Yugoslavia, Italy, Singapore and New Zealand, and lived for short periods in Europe, Asia and New Zealand. He currently lives in Melbourne.

The Silent Piano Fremantle Arts Centre Press, 1980.
The Projectionist Fremantle Arts Centre Press, 1983.
Sky Poems Fremantle Arts Centre Press, 1987; 1993.
Barbecue of the Primitives UQP, 1989.
Tremors, Pamphlet Poets Series #2 National Library of Australia, 1991.
Feeding the Ghost Penguin, 1993.
The Rome Air Naked Penguin, 1996.
New and Selected Poems Fremantle Arts Centre Press, 1998.

Andrew Sant was born in London in 1950, where he lived until coming with his family to Australia in 1962. He is a graduate of La Trobe University, has travelled widely, and is a former editor of the literary quarterly, *Island*, which he co-founded in 1979. He has worked as a boatman, manager of a hostel for delinquent youth and, more recently, as a teacher at both secondary and tertiary levels. Since his first book he has received several Australia Council grants, and his residencies include a period at the B R Whiting Library in Rome. With Caroline Evans he has two daughters, Freya and Leah.

Lives Angus & Robertson, 1980.
The Caught Sky Angus & Robertson, 1982.
The Flower Industry Angus & Robertson, 1985.
Brushing the Dark Heinemann, 1989.
Album of Domestic Exiles Black Pepper, 1997.

Andrew Taylor is the author of eleven books of poetry, two opera libretti, numerous articles and the critical study, *Reading Australian Poetry* (1987). His book *Sandstone* won the Western Australian Premier's Prize, while *Travelling* was the regional winner of the British Airways Commonwealth Poetry Prize. Educated at Melbourne University, he taught for many years at the University of Adelaide. He was Chairperson of two Writers' Weeks at the Adelaide Festival of Arts. He has lived extensively in Europe and the United States, and is currently Foundation Professor of English at Edith Cowan University in Western Australia.

Travelling UQP, 1986.
Selected Poems 1960-1985 UQP, 1988.
Folds in the Map UQP, 1991.
Sandstone UQP, 1995.

John **Tranter** spent his youth on a farm on the south-east coast of
Australia. He attended country schools, and took his Bachelor of
Arts in 1970 after attending university sporadically. He has worked
mainly in publishing and radio production for the ABC, and has
travelled widely, making reading tours of the United States,
England and Europe in recent years. He has received several senior
fellowships and other grants from the Literature Board of the
Australia Council. His work appears in the *Norton Anthology of
Modern Poetry*. He edited the *Penguin Book of Modern Australian
Poetry*, published in Britain and the USA as the *Bloodaxe Book of
Modern Australian Poetry*, and is the editor of the free Internet
magazine *Jacket* (http://www.jacket.zip.com.au/welcome.html).

Parallax South Head Press, 1970 (published as *Poetry Australia*
   magazine, number 34, June 1970).
Red Movie and other poems Angus & Robertson, 1972.
The Blast Area Makar Press, 1974.
The Alphabet Murders (notes from a work in progress) Angus &
   Robertson, 1976.
Crying in Early Infancy — 100 Sonnets Makar Press, 1977.
Dazed in the Ladies Lounge Island Press, 1979.
Selected Poems Hale & Iremonger, 1982.
Under Berlin UQP, 1988.
The Floor of Heaven Angus & Robertson/HarperCollins, 1992.
At The Florida UQP, 1993.
Gasoline Kisses Equipage, UK, 1997.
Late Night Radio Polygon Press, UK, 1998.

Chris **Wallace-Crabbe** was born in Melbourne in 1934. He has published a number of critical books: *Melbourne or the Bush* (1974), *Toil &
Spin* (1979), and *Falling Into Language* (1990). His other books include
the anthology *The Golden Apples of The Sun* (1980) and the novel
Splinters (1981). He was elected a Fellow of the Australian Academy
of Humanities in 1984, and has taught at universities around the
world — including Melbourne, Venice and Harvard. From
1989–1994 he was director of the Australian Centre at the University
of Melbourne.

The Music of Division Angus & Robertson, 1959.
In Light and Darkness Angus & Robertson, 1963.
The Rebel General Angus & Robertson, 1967.
Where The Wind Came Angus & Robertson, 1971.
The Foundations of Joy Angus & Robertson, 1976.
Emotions Are Not Skilled Workers Angus & Robertson, 1980.

The Amorous Cannibal Oxford University Press, 1985.
I'm Deadly Serious Oxford University Press, 1988.
For Crying Out Loud Oxford University Press, 1990.
Rungs of Time Oxford University Press, 1993.
Selected Poems 1956-1994 Oxford University Press, 1995.
Whirling Oxford University Press, 1998.

Alan Wearne has been part of Australian poetry since his Monash University days (1967–68). Added to the poets mentioned in his statement he finds he returns to Juvenal, Shakespeare, Marvell, Dryden, Gray, Tennyson, Clough, Baudelaire, Hardy, Kipling, Frost, Pessoa, Slessor, Drummond de Andrade, Auden, MacNeice, Kees, Larkin, Koch, O'Hara, Baxter, Haavikko and Berrigan. Gig Ryan, Nigel Roberts and Pi O are his closest colleagues. As well as poetry he has written a detective/fantasy/farce/satire on Melbourne and its footy, *Kicking in Danger* (1997). His one intellectual love being history (anything from the big bang onward), he is a graduate in that subject from LaTrobe University.

Public Relations Makar Press, 1972.
New Devil, New Parish UQP, 1976.
The Nightmarkets Penguin, 1986.
Out Here Bloodaxe Books, UK, 1987.
The Lovemakers Penguin, 1999.

Fay Zwicky. Born in Melbourne, she pursued a career as a concert pianist and university teacher before becoming a full-time human in 1987. She has published five collections of poetry — *Kaddish and Other Poems* winning the NSW Premier's Award in 1982, *Ask Me*, the Western Australian Premier's Award in 1991, and *The Gatekeeper's Wife* the Western Australian Premier's Award (jointly) in 1999. A widely-acclaimed short story collection, *Hostages*, was published in 1983. Subsequent stories have appeared spasmodically in Australian and overseas journals and anthologies, and have been translated into many languages.

Isaac Babel's Fiddle Maximus, 1975.
Kaddish and Other Poems UQP, 1982.
Ask Me UQP, 1990.
Poems 1970–1992 UQP, 1993.
The Gatekeeper's Wife Brandl & Schlesinger, 1997.